CHENG & TSUI

"Bringing Asia to the World"™

中文听说读写 · 中文聽說讀寫

INTEGRATED CHINESE

Simplified and Traditional Characters

3

Workbook

4th Edition

Yuehua Liu and Tao-chung Yao
Liangyan Ge, Nyan-Ping Bi, Yaohua Shi

Original Edition by Yuehua Liu and Tao-chung Yao
Nyan-Ping Bi and Yaohua Shi

CHENG & TSUI

"Bringing Asia to the World"™

Copyright © 2018, 2009, 2005, 1997 by
Cheng & Tsui Company, Inc.

Fourth Edition 2018

27 26 25 24 23 22   5 6 7 8 9 10

ISBN 978-1-62291-157-8 [Fourth Edition,
Simplified and Traditional Characters]

Printed in the United States of America

The *Integrated Chinese* series encompasses
textbooks, workbooks, character workbooks,
teacher's resources, audio, video, and more.
Content is available in a variety of formats,
including print and online via the ChengTsui
Web App™. Visit chengtsui.co for more
information on the other components of
Integrated Chinese.

Publisher
JILL CHENG

Editorial Manager
BEN SHRAGGE

Editors
MIKE YONG and LIJIE QIN

Creative Director
CHRISTIAN SABOGAL

Interior Designers
LIZ YATES with KATE PAPADAKI

Illustrator
KATE PAPADAKI

Cheng & Tsui Company, Inc.
25 West Street
Boston, MA 02111-1213 USA
Phone (617) 988-2400 / (800) 554-1963
Fax (617) 426-3669
chengtsui.co

Contents

Preface

In designing the workbook exercises for Volumes 3 and 4 of *Integrated Chinese* (IC), we sought to give equal emphasis to the core language skills of listening, speaking, reading, and writing. For the new edition, we have also added *pinyin* and tone exercises for students to progressively improve their pronunciation and lesson opener checklists for them to track their learning. Where appropriate, we have labeled the exercises as interpretive, interpersonal, or presentational according to the American Council on the Teaching of Foreign Languages (ACTFL) *21st Century Skills Map for World Languages*.

In addition to the print editions, the IC workbooks are also available online through the **ChengTsui Web App™** (*Essential* and *Educator Editions*). In the digital format, the exercises are presented alongside the textbook content, and automatic feedback for students is provided. For more information about the Web App, visit chengtsui.co.

Organizational Principles

As with the textbooks, the IC Volume 3 and 4 workbooks do not follow one pedagogical methodology, but instead blend several effective teaching approaches. In addition, the full text is offered in both simplified and traditional characters, with simplified characters appearing first. When accessed through the ChengTsui Web App, the workbooks are particularly suited for differentiated instruction, blended learning, and the flipped classroom. Here are some features that distinguish the IC workbooks:

Form and Function

The ultimate purpose of learning any language is to be able to communicate in that language. With that goal in mind, we pay equal attention to language form and function. In addition to traditional workbook exercise types (e.g., fill-in-the-blanks, sentence completion, translation, multiple choice), we include task-based assignments that equip students to handle real-life situations using accurate and appropriate language. These exercises provide linguistic context and are written to reflect idiomatic usage.

Visual Learning

Engaging learners through rich visuals is key to our pedagogy. To build a bridge between the classroom and the target language setting, we include a range of exercises centered on authentic materials. We also include illustration-based exercises that prompt students to answer questions directly in Chinese without going through the process of translation.

Learner-Centered Tasks

We believe that workbook exercises should not only align with the textbook, but also relate to students' lives. We include exercises that simulate daily life and reference culturally relevant topics and themes, including social media and globalization. We hope such open-ended exercises will actively engage students in the subject matter, and keep them interested in the language-learning process.

Differentiated Instruction

We have designed the exercises at different difficulty levels to suit varying curricular needs. Therefore, teachers should assign the exercises at their discretion; they may use some or all of them, in any sequence. Moreover, teachers may complement the workbook exercises with their own materials.

Bringing It Together

Every five lessons, we provide a short cumulative review unit ("Bringing It Together") for students who wish to check their progress. These flexible units do not introduce any new learning materials, and can be included in or excluded from curricula according to individual needs.

The exercises in this workbook have been designed to recycle vocabulary learned and provide a contextualized language environment.

The workbook lesson sections are as follows:

Listening Comprehension

All too often, listening comprehension is sacrificed in the formal classroom setting. Because of time constraints, students tend to focus their time and energy on mastering a few grammar points. We include a substantial number of listening comprehension exercises to remedy this imbalance. There are two categories of listening exercises; both can be done on students' own time or in the classroom. In either case, the instructor should review students' answers for accuracy.

The first group of listening exercises, which is placed at the beginning of this section, is based on the scenarios in the lesson. For the exercises to be meaningful, students should study the vocabulary list before listening to the recordings.

The second group of listening exercises is based on audio recordings of two or more short dialogues or narratives. These exercises are designed to give students extra practice on the vocabulary and grammar points introduced in the lesson. The Workbook Listening Rejoinder exercises are significantly more difficult than others. These exercises should be assigned towards the end of the lesson, after students have familiarized themselves with its content. For the Fourth Edition, these exercises have largely been reworked as multiple-choice or true/false questions to facilitate easy assessment.

Audio for the workbooks (and textbooks) is accessible via the ChengTsui Web App and, for print users, at chengtsui.co/resources.

Pinyin and Tone

To solidify students' grasp of the finer points of Mandarin pronunciation, this section incorporates exercises that focus specifically on comparing and distinguishing initials, finals, and tones, as well as on differentiating characters that have more than one pronunciation.

Speaking

As with Listening Comprehension, this section includes two groups of exercises. They should be assigned separately based on students' proficiency level.

To help students apply new vocabulary and grammar knowledge to meaningful communication, we first ask questions related to the Lesson Text, and then ask questions related to their own lives. These questions require a one- or two-sentence answer. By stringing together short questions and answers, students can construct their own dialogues, practice in pairs, or take turns asking or answering questions.

As their confidence increases, students can progress to more difficult prompts that invite them to express opinions on a number of topics. Some of these topics are abstract, so they gradually teach students to express their opinions in longer conversations or statements. As the school year progresses, these speaking exercises should take up more class discussion time. Because this second group of exercises can be challenging, it should be attempted only after students are well grounded in the lesson's grammar and vocabulary. Usually, this does not occur immediately after students have completed the first group of exercises.

Reading Comprehension

To help students understand how their newly acquired vocabulary and grammatical structures function in meaningful contexts, this section includes questions asking students to match terms, answer questions in English or Chinese, or answer multiple-choice questions based on readings. There are also activities based on realia. There are two types of reading exercises in the workbook: short passages incorporating new vocabulary and grammar structures from the lesson, and authentic materials such as advertisements, personal ads, and short news articles.

Writing and Grammar

As the culmination of each lesson, this section includes exercises that enable students to consolidate what they have just learned.

While training students to work on their proficiency at the sentence and paragraph levels, we saw a need to help students solidify their foundation in character recognition and word association. Hence, character- and word-building exercises are included in each lesson.

Open-ended prompts and exercises are provided to cement students' grasp of important grammar points. Through brief exchanges, students answer questions using specific grammatical forms, or are given sentences to complete. Because they must provide context for these exercises, students cannot treat them as simple mechanical repetition drills.

Translation has been an age-old tool for language teaching and still has its place today. Positive student feedback confirms our belief in its continued importance. The translation exercises we have devised serve two primary functions: one, to have students apply specific grammatical structures; and two, to encourage students to build their vocabulary. Ultimately, we believe this dual-pronged approach will enable students to realize that it takes more than just literal translation to convey an idea in a foreign language.

We have also included exercises that encourage students to express themselves through writing. Many of the topics overlap with those used in oral practice, and we expect that students will find it easier to write what they have already learned to express orally.

Finally, to train students to tell a complete story based on what they see and use their language skills to construct narratives, an illustrated storytelling exercise is provided at the end of each lesson. These exercises require students to draw on what they have just learned in order to recount the story depicted.

Note: Prefaces to previous editions of IC are available at chengtsui.co.

Lesson 1

第一课

第一課

开学 開學

Starting a New Semester

✓ Check off the following language functions as you learn how to:

[ ] Ask and answer questions about where you were born and grew up

[ ] Discuss whether you prefer to live on or off campus

[ ] Express a dissenting view politely

As you progress through the lesson, note other language functions you would like to learn.

_____

_____

_____

I. Listening Comprehension

Audio

A Listen to the Textbook audio, then circle the most appropriate choice. INTERPRETIVE

1 **Zhang Tianming is a**
   a freshman.
   b sophomore.
   c junior.
   d senior.

2 **How did Zhang Tianming get to campus?**
   a by bus and subway
   b by train and taxi
   c by airplane and taxi
   d by train and bus

3 **Ke Lin is a**
   a teacher.
   b graduate student.
   c senior.
   d junior.

B Based on the Textbook audio, mark these statements true or false. INTERPRETIVE

1 ____ **Ke Lin lives in a dorm on campus.**

2 ____ **Ke Lin offers to help Zhang Tianming move into his dorm.**

3 ____ **Ke Lin takes Zhang Tianming's computer by mistake.**

C Listen to the Workbook Dialogue audio, then mark these statements true or false. INTERPRETIVE

1 ____ **The dialogue takes place in front of a freshman dorm.**

2 ____ **The man knows the university's campus very well because he is a senior there.**

3 ____ **The woman was on a plane earlier today.**

4 ____ **The dorm has been for returning students for years.**

5 ____ **The taxi driver has dropped off the woman in the wrong place.**

6 ____ **The man lives on the west side of the freshman dorm.**

D Listen to the Workbook Narrative 1 audio, then mark these statements true or false. INTERPRETIVE

1 ____ *"Zhù xiào"* **means "to live off campus."**

2 ____ **Both** *"shìyoǔ"* **and** *"tóngwū"* **mean "roommate."**

E Listen to the Workbook Narrative 2 audio, then mark these statements true or false. INTERPRETIVE

1 _____ Little Wang wants to move out of his dorm because it's too noisy.

2 _____ Little Wang's new place is very close to campus.

3 _____ Little Wang shares his new apartment with his old roommate.

F Listen to the Workbook Narrative 3 audio, then fill out the blanks between the images with Little Zhang's activities in Chinese. Finally, answer the questions in English. INTERPRETIVE & PRESENTATIONAL

1

_____

_____

_____

_____

_____

_____

_____

_____

_____

_____

2 For how long does Little Zhang listen to audio recordings every day?

_____

3 How many classes does Little Zhang have every day?

_____

4 Where does Little Zhang access the Internet?

_____

G Listen to the Workbook Narrative 4 audio, then write down the two names in Chinese characters.
INTERPRETIVE & PRESENTATIONAL

1 _____   2 _____

H ____ Listen to the Workbook Listening Rejoinder audio. After hearing the first speaker, select the best response from the four choices given by the second speaker. Indicate the letter of your choice. INTERPRETIVE

II. Pinyin and Tone

A Compare the pronunciations of the underlined characters in the two words or phrases given. Provide their initials in *pinyin*.

长大/長大 _____   弓长张/弓長張 _____

B Compare the tones of the underlined characters in the two words or phrases given. Indicate the tones with 1 (first tone), 2 (second tone), 3 (third tone), 4 (fourth tone), or 0 (neutral tone).

适应/適應 _____   应该/應該 _____

III. Speaking

A To get to know your Chinese language partner/classmate better, ask the following questions in Chinese and report the information gathered. INTERPERSONAL & PRESENTATIONAL

1 What's your name?

2 Where are you from?

3 Where were you born?

4 Where did you grow up?

5 Are you a college freshman?

6 Do you live on or off campus? Do you like where you live? Why or why not?

7 How long have you been studying Chinese?

8 Do you have a Chinese name? If so, how do you write it?

B Practice asking and answering these questions. INTERPERSONAL

1 你是在什么地方出生的？

你是在什麼地方出生的？

2 你是在什么地方长大的？

你是在什麼地方長大的？

3 你今天是几点到的教室？

你今天是幾點到的教室？

4 你今天是怎么来的学校？走路，开车，还是坐公共汽车？

你今天是怎麼來的學校？走路，開車，還是坐公共汽車？

5 学校是几号开学的？

學校是幾號開學的？

6 你住校内还是住校外？

你住校內還是住校外？

7 要是你有钱，你想搬到什么地方去住？为什么？

要是你有錢，你想搬到什麼地方去住？為什麼？

Practice speaking with these prompts. **PRESENTATIONAL**

1 请你介绍一下你自己。

请你介绍一下你自己。

2 请你谈一谈你上大学（or 高中）的第一天在学校里都做了些什么。

請你談一談你上大學（or 高中）的第一天在學校裡都做了些什麼。

3 你觉得住在学校宿舍好，还是住在校外好？为什么？

你覺得住在學校宿舍好，還是住在校外好？為什麼？

IV. Reading Comprehension

A Complete this section by writing the characters, *pinyin*, and English equivalent of each new word formed. Guess the meaning, then use a dictionary to confirm. **INTERPRETIVE**

1 "卫生间"的"卫生" + "一张纸"的"纸"

"衛生間"的"衛生" + "一張紙"的"紙"

→ 卫生/衛生 + 纸/紙→ _____ _____ _____

2 "帮忙"的"帮" + "手"

"幫忙"的"幫" + "手"

→ 帮/幫 + 手→ _____ _____ _____

3 "学校"的"校" + "公园"的"园"

"學校"的"校" + "公園"的"園"

→ 校+园/園→ _____ _____ _____

4 "吃坏肚子"的"坏" + "好处"的"处"

"吃壞肚子"的"壞" + "好處"的"處"

→ 坏/壞+处/處→ _____ _____ _____

林明： 哎，王新！你怎么又搬家了？你上个学期
刚刚从校内搬到校外，现在又要搬回学校
宿舍了？

王新： 住在宿舍的时候觉得房租太贵，而且不自
由。可是住在校外很不方便。上个星期三
早上我考试又去晚了，觉得还是搬回宿舍
好，所以就搬回来了。

林明： 你不会在学校宿舍住两个月，又想搬到校
外去吧？

王新： 说真的，住在宿舍又方便又安全，可是一
到周末我还是会想起住在校外的好处：房
租便宜得多，而且很自由。

林明： 我有个好办法。你可以租两套房子，一套
在校内，一套在校外。你星期一到星期五
住在校内，一到周末就住到校外去。这样
你会觉得又方便又安全，而且自由。

王新： 你这个办法很有意思。要是我有钱，那真
是个好办法。

林明： 哎，王新！你怎麼又搬家了？你上個學期
剛剛從校內搬到校外，現在又要搬回學校
宿舍了？

王新： 住在宿舍的時候覺得房租太貴，而且不自
由。可是住在校外很不方便。上個星期三
早上我考試又去晚了，覺得還是搬回宿舍
好，所以就搬回來了。

林明： 你不會在學校宿舍住兩個月，又想搬到校
外去吧？

王新：說真的，住在宿舍又方便又安全，可是一
　　　到週末我還是會想起住在校外的好處：房
　　　租便宜得多，而且很自由。

林明：我有個好辦法。你可以租兩套房子，一套
　　　在校內，一套在校外。你星期一到星期五
　　　住在校內，一到週末就住到校外去。這樣
　　　你會覺得又方便又安全，而且自由。

王新：你這個辦法很有意思。要是我有錢，那真
　　　是個好辦法。

1 ____ Wang Xin has been living in the dorms for a semester.

2 ____ Lin Ming thinks Wang Xin has moved too many times.

3 ____ One of the reasons that Wang Xin moved out of the dorms was that it was too expensive.

4 ____ Wang Xin had never been late for a test until last Wednesday.

5 ____ It was not easy for Wang Xin to decide to move again.

6 ____ Wang Xin has already decided to move yet again in two months.

7 ____ Lin Ming doesn't think Wang Xin can make up his mind where he wants to live.

8 ____ According to Wang Xin, it is much less expensive to live off campus.

9 ____ If Wang Xin follows Lin Ming's suggestion, he will be able to save money.

C Review Zhang Tianming's schedule and complete the passage accordingly. INTERPRETIVE

早上　　　起床/起床

　　　　　吃早饭/吃早飯

　　　　　上中文课/上中文課

　　　　　上电脑课/上電腦課

　　　　　上网/上網

下午　　　吃午饭/吃午飯

　　　　　上音乐课/上音樂課

　　　　　打球

　　　　　回宿舍

晚上　　　吃晚饭/吃晚飯

　　　　　做功课/做功課

　　　　　看电视/看電視

　　　　　睡觉/睡覺

　　张天明今天早上_____以后，很快地吃了点儿早
饭，就去上中文课。_____，没能休息，就
去上电脑课。_____，他到图书馆去____。
吃午饭的时候，柯林坐在他的旁边。柯林说："我今
天有四节课，已经上了三节了，你呢？"张天明回答说：
"我_____，还有一节音乐课。"下午回宿舍
前，张天明跟朋友去____。_____，才回宿舍吃晚饭。
张天明今天的功课不多，____一个钟头就_____。然
后，____半个钟头的电视，就上床睡觉了。

　　張天明今天早上_____以後，很快地吃了點兒早
飯，就去上中文課。_____，沒能休息，就
去上電腦課。_____，他到圖書館去____。
吃午飯的時候，柯林坐在他的旁邊。柯林說："我今
天有四節課，已經上了三節了，你呢？"張天明回答說：
"我_____，還有一節音樂課。"下午回宿舍
前，張天明跟朋友去____。_____，才回宿舍吃晚飯。
張天明今天的功課不多，____一個鐘頭就_____。然
後，____半個鐘頭的電視，就上床睡覺了。

中国人民大学
RENMIN UNIVERSITY OF CHINA
对外语言文化学院

李 泉 博士 教授
世界汉语教学学会理事
中国对外汉语教学学会常务理事
全国汉语国际教育硕士专业教指委委员

中国·北京海淀区中关村大街59号
邮编: 100872
电话: 010-6251xxxx
传真: 010-8250xxxx
电邮: xxxxx@ruc.edu.cn

中國人民大學
RENMIN UNIVERSITY OF CHINA
對外語言文化學院

李 泉 博士 教授
世界漢語教學學會理事
中國對外漢語教學學會常務理事
全國漢語國際教育碩士專業教指委委員
中國·北京海淀區中關村大街59號
郵編: 100872
電話: 010-6251xxxx
傳真: 010-8250xxxx
電郵: xxxxx@ruc.edu.cn

1 这个人姓什么？

這個人姓什麼？

a 李

b 博

c 教

2 他在哪一个城市工作？

　他在哪一個城市工作？

　　a　海淀

　　b　北京

　　c　中关村／中關村

3 他是做什么的？

　他是做什麼的？

　　a　老师／老師

　　b　医生／醫生

　　c　律师／律師

V. Writing and Grammar

A Form a character by combining the given components as indicated. Then use that character to write a word, phrase, or short sentence.

1 左边一个"车"，右边一个"两"，

　左邊一個"車"，右邊一個"兩"，

　是 ＿＿＿＿＿＿ 的 ＿＿＿＿ 。

2 上边一个"少"，下边一个"目"，

　上邊一個"少"，下邊一個"目"，

　是 ＿＿＿＿＿＿ 的 ＿＿＿＿ 。

3 左边一个"弓"，右边一个"长"，

　左邊一個"弓"，右邊一個"長"，

　是 ＿＿＿＿＿＿ 的 ＿＿＿＿ 。

4 左边一个"木"，右边一个"可"，

　左邊一個"木"，右邊一個"可"，

　是 ＿＿＿＿＿＿ 的 ＿＿＿＿ 。

Answer the questions based on your own circumstances. **INTERPERSONAL**

1 Q: 学校开学几天了？
　　學校開學幾天了？

　　A: _____

2 Q: 你学中文学了几个学期了？
　　你學中文學了幾個學期了？

　　A: _____

3 Q: 每天吃完晚饭以后，你做什么？
　　每天吃完晚飯以後，你做什麼？

　　A: _____

C Answer the questions based on your own circumstances. **INTERPERSONAL**

1 Q: 你今天是几点起的床？
　　你今天是幾點起的床？

　　A: _____

2 Q: 你今天是几点去上课的？
　　你今天是幾點去上課的？

　　A: _____

3 Q: 你今天是怎么去上课的？
　　你今天是怎麼去上課的？

　　A: _____

4 Q: 你的电脑是在哪儿买的？什么时候买的？
　　你的電腦是在哪兒買的？什麼時候買的？

　　A: _____

Answer the questions based on your own circumstances. INTERPERSONAL

1 Q: 你这个学期除了上中文课以外，还上什么课？
你這個學期除了上中文課以外，還上什麼課？

A: _____

2 Q: 你除了会说中文以外，还会说什么外语？
你除了會說中文以外，還會說什麼外語？

A: _____

3 Q: 你的房间除了床以外，还有什么家具？
你的房間除了床以外，還有什麼傢俱？

A: _____

4 Q: 这个周末除了学习、做功课以外，你还打算做什么？
這個週末除了學習、做功課以外，你還打算做什麼？

A: _____

E Let's get to know Ke Lin. Using the 除了…以外，都 structure, answer the questions based on the information given, following the example below. INTERPRETIVE & PRESENTATIONAL

星期一	星期二	星期三	星期四	星期五	星期六	星期日
✗	✗	✓	✓	✓	✓	✓

Q: 柯林星期几有空？
柯林星期幾有空？

A: 柯林除了星期一、星期二以外，别的时间都有空。
柯林除了星期一、星期二以外，別的時間都有空。

1

✓	✓	✓	✓	✗

Q: 柯林喜欢什么运动?
柯林喜歡什麼運動?

A: _____

2

Beijing	London	New York	Tokyo	Paris	Sydney
✗	✓	✓	✓	✓	✓

Q: 柯林去过哪些城市?
柯林去過哪些城市?

A: _____

3

✗	✓	✗	✗	✗

Q: 柯林不喜欢喝什么饮料?
柯林不喜歡喝什麼飲料?

A: _____

F Answer the questions, then explain your answers based on the Lesson Text or your own circumstances, following the example below. INTERPERSONAL

Q: 张天明为什么住在学校宿舍里?
張天明為什麼住在學校宿舍裡?

A: 因为可以适应学校生活，再说上课也方便。
因為可以適應學校生活，再說上課也方便。

1 Q: 你为什么学中文？
    你為什麼學中文？

    A: _____

2 Q: 你为什么上这个学校？
    你為什麼上這個學校？

    A: _____

3 Q: 柯林为什么住在校外？
    柯林為什麼住在校外？

    A: _____

G Complete these sentences using 不见得/不見得, following the example below. **INTERPERSONAL**

Person A: 他父母是中国人，虽然他是在美国长大的，但是学中文应该很容易吧？
           他父母是中國人，雖然他是在美國長大的，但是學中文應該很容易吧？

Person B: 在美国长大的中国孩子，学中文不见得容易。
           在美國長大的中國孩子，學中文不見得容易。

1 Person A: 这个宿舍很贵，我真想搬出去住。
             這個宿舍很貴，我真想搬出去住。

   Person B: 很多校外的房子也很贵，_____。
             很多校外的房子也很貴，_____。

2 Person A: 你们这个宿舍很安静，下个学期我打算搬进来。
             你們這個宿舍很安靜，下個學期我打算搬進來。

   Person B: 这个宿舍房间不多，好像都有人住，

             _____。

             這個宿舍房間不多，好像都有人住，

             _____。

3 Person A: 他是老生，我们有什么事都可以去问他。

他是老生，我們有什麼事都可以去問他。

Person B: 他只比我们早来一年，＿＿＿＿＿＿＿＿＿＿。

他只比我們早來一年，＿＿＿＿＿＿＿＿＿＿。

H Zhang Tianming can be scatterbrained. Based on the illustrations, imagine what he would say upon realizing he has left something behind, following the example below. PRESENTATIONAL

糟糕，我把电脑拉在出租车上了。

糟糕，我把電腦拉在出租車上了。

1

_____

2

_____

3

_____

I Fill in the blanks using the words or phrases given, then answer the question using 第一…，第二…，第三….INTERPRETIVE

除了　　以外　　因为　　再说

　　王健是在北京出生，在北京长大的。高中毕业以后，他父母就叫他到这个大学来留学。王健问爸爸为什么要来这个大学？爸爸说："_____这个大学很有名，老师很好。_____学校有名、老师好_____，听说从这个学校毕业的学生找工作也容易。_____，你阿姨就住在这个城市，周末你可以去阿姨家吃中国饭，就不会很想家，能快一点儿适应在美国的生活。"

除了　　以外　　因為　　再說

　　王健是在北京出生，在北京長大的。高中畢業以後，他父母就叫他到這個大學來留學。王健問爸爸為什麼要來這個大學？爸爸說："_____這個大學很有名，老師很好。_____學校有名、老師好_____，聽說從這個學校畢業的學生找工作也容易。_____，你阿姨就住在這個城市，週末你可以去阿姨家吃中國飯，就不會很想家，能快一點兒適應在美國的生活。"

王健的爸爸为什么叫他来这个大学学习？
王健的爸爸為什麼叫他來這個大學學習？

J Translate these sentences into Chinese. PRESENTATIONAL

1 Q: When will school start?

_____

A: Next Wednesday.

_____

2 Q: What time did you get home yesterday?

_____

A: I got home at 10:30 p.m.

_____

3 Q: Did you go to New York by plane or by car?

_____

A: I went by car.

_____

4 Person A: Living in the dorms is very convenient.

_____

Person B: But it doesn't necessarily save you money.

_____

K Translate these passages into Chinese. PRESENTATIONAL

1 That first-year student was born in China, but raised in the U.S. I helped her move into her dorm yesterday. Her parents want her to live in the dorms to get used to college life, but she feels that living in the dorms is too restrictive and wants to live off campus next semester.

_____

_____

_____

2 Zhang Tianming got to know a new friend this morning. His name is Ke Lin. Zhang Tianming met Ke Lin in his dorm. There were many people in the dorm; except for Ke Lin, Zhang Tianming didn't know anyone. Ke Lin helped Zhang Tianming move his stuff. After helping him move, Ke Lin said to Zhang Tianming, "If you need any help, call me."

_____

_____

_____

_____

3 Little Zhang is from China. He moved to the U.S. just last year. He has been living in California for more than a year, yet he still hasn't adapted to life in the U.S. He thinks that it's really inconvenient to live in the U.S. without a car. He often has to ask other people to take him shopping. Next semester, he'd like to buy a car and help new students.

_____

_____

_____

_____

L Describe your first day at the school you attend now. Include information such as when and how you got to school, which classmates or dormmates you met that day, and (if relevant) whether you liked your living quarters and why. PRESENTATIONAL

_____

_____

_____

_____

M Write a story in Chinese based on the four images below. Make sure that your story has a beginning, middle, and end, and that the transition from one picture to the next is smooth and logical. PRESENTATIONAL

1

2

3

4

_____

_____

_____

_____

_____

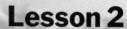

宿舍生活

Dorm Life

 Check off the following language functions as you learn how to:

[ ] Name the furniture in your room

[ ] Describe your living quarters

[ ] Comment on someone's living quarters

[ ] Present opinions tactfully

As you progress through the lesson, note other language functions you would like to learn.

_____

_____

_____

I. Listening Comprehension

Audio

A | Listen to the Lesson Text audio, then mark these statements true or false. INTERPRETIVE

1 ____ Zhang Tianming moved into his dorm before his roommate.

2 ____ Their room is close to a main road.

B | Based on the Lesson Text audio, circle the most appropriate choice. INTERPRETIVE

1 **Zhang Tianming and his roommate each have**

a   a desk, a chair, a bed, a wardrobe, and a bookshelf.

b   a desk, a bed, a bookshelf, a sofa, and a wardrobe.

c   a bookshelf, a bed, a dining table, a chair, and a wardrobe.

2 **What are the advantages of Zhang Tianming's dorm?**

a   It is quiet, spacious, and close to the classrooms.

b   It is conveniently located and nicely air-conditioned.

c   It is quiet and conveniently located.

3 **What are the disadvantages of Zhang Tianming's dorm?**

a   It is old and noisy, and the food in the cafeteria is bad.

b   It is old with no air conditioning, and the food in the cafeteria is bad.

c   There are no washing machines, and the food in the cafeteria is bad.

C | Listen to the Workbook Dialogue audio, then mark these statements true or false. INTERPRETIVE

1 ____ Daming's building is located in a quiet environment.

2 ____ Daming does not like his dorm room.

3 ____ Daming's friend lives in the same dorm but on a different floor.

4 ____ Daming will most likely continue to live in the dorm for the rest of the semester.

D | Based on the Workbook Dialogue audio, circle the most appropriate choice. INTERPRETIVE

1 **When is Daming's room quietest?**

a   from one o'clock p.m. to four o'clock p.m.

b   from four o'clock p.m. to seven o'clock p.m.

c   from seven o'clock p.m. to ten o'clock p.m.

2 **According to Daming, what is the main source of the noise?**

a   over fifty students who live on the same floor

b   traffic on the major road outside

c   one of the dryers in the laundry room

E   Listen to the Workbook Narrative 1 audio, then write down the characters described. INTERPRETIVE

1 _____   2 _____

F   Listen to the Workbook Narrative 2 audio, then circle the most appropriate choice. INTERPRETIVE

1   The room has

    a   a desk, a wardrobe, a bed, a bookshelf, and two chairs.

    b   a bed, a bookshelf, a chair, a desk, and a couch.

    c   a bookshelf, a desk, a wardrobe, a sofa, and a bed.

2   What does the narrator like about his room?

    a   It is close to the library and convenient for dining.

    b   It is close to the classrooms, the laundry room, and the library.

    c   It is close to the classrooms and convenient for dining and doing laundry.

3   What is the room's only shortcoming?

    a   It has no closets.

    b   It has no windows.

    c   It has no dining table.

G   Listen to Workbook Narrative 3.

1   Draw a picture of Little Li's room. INTERPRETIVE

2   In Chinese, answer the question at the end of the audio. INTERPERSONAL

_____

H   ____   Listen to the Workbook Listening Rejoinder audio. After hearing the first speaker, select the best response from the four choices given by the second speaker. Indicate the letter of your choice. INTERPRETIVE

A Compare the pronunciations of the underlined characters in the two words or phrases given. Provide their finals in *pinyin*.

摆<u>着</u>/擺<u>著</u> _____　　　　<u>着</u>急/<u>著</u>急 _____

B Compare the tones of the underlined characters in the two words/phrases given. Indicate the tones with 1 (first tone), 2 (second tone), 3 (third tone), 4 (fourth tone), or 0 (neutral tone).

有<u>空</u>儿/有<u>空</u>兒 _____　　　　<u>空</u>调/<u>空</u>調 _____

III. Speaking

A Practice asking and answering these questions. **INTERPERSONAL**

1 你的房间里有什么家具？

   你的房間裡有什麼傢俱？

2 你的书桌上摆着一些什么东西？

   你的書桌上擺著一些什麼東西？

3 你住的地方离学校哪一栋楼最近？

   你住的地方離學校哪一棟樓最近？

4 你去过的中国餐馆儿，哪一家的菜最地道？

   你去過的中國餐館兒，哪一家的菜最地道？

B Practice speaking on these topics. **INTERPERSONAL**

1 你的房间（我现在住在……）

   你的房間（我現在住在……）

2 你喜欢什么样的房间？

   你喜歡什麼樣的房間？

C Describe this room in detail. PRESENTATIONAL

IV. Reading Comprehension

A Write the characters, *pinyin*, and English equivalent of each new word formed. Guess the meaning, then use a dictionary to confirm.

1 "商店"的"商"＋"日用品"的"品"

→ 商 ＋ 品→ _____ _____ _____

2 "出去玩"的"玩"＋"文具"的"具"

→ 玩 ＋ 具→ _____ _____ _____

3 "挂衣服"的"挂"+"号码"的"号"

　"掛衣服"的"掛"+"號碼"的"號"

　→ 挂/掛 ＋ 号/號→ ＿＿＿＿ ＿＿＿＿ ＿＿＿＿

4 "同屋"的"同"+"什么事"的"事"

　"同屋"的"同"+"什麼事"的"事"

　→ 同 ＋ 事→ ＿＿＿＿ ＿＿＿＿ ＿＿＿＿

5 "地方"的"地"+"毯子"的"毯"

　→ 地 ＋ 毯→ ＿＿＿＿ ＿＿＿＿ ＿＿＿＿

B The following excerpt is part of a dialogue between a landlord and a potential tenant. Read it and answer the questions in English. **INTERPRETIVE**

Person A: 对不起，请问，房间里有空调吗？

Person B: 没有。这儿一般不热。

Person A: 卫生间大不大？

Person B: 一个人用，没问题。

Person A: 这栋楼旧不旧？

Person B: 不是很旧，二十几年。

Person A: 离马路近吗？

Person B: 很远。这儿很安静。

Person A: 有没有洗衣机和干衣机？

Person B: 没有，可是离洗衣服的地方不远。

Person A: 我不喜欢做饭，附近有饭馆儿吗？

Person B: 有，旁边有一家很地道的中国饭馆儿。

Person A: 房租多少钱？

Person B: 每个月四百块。

Person A: 對不起，請問，房間裡有空調嗎？

Person B: 沒有。這兒一般不熱。

Person A: 衛生間大不大？

Person B: 一個人用，沒問題。

Person A: 這棟樓舊不舊？

Person B: 不是很舊，二十幾年。

Person A: 離馬路近嗎？

Person B: 很遠。這兒很安靜。

Person A: 有沒有洗衣機和乾衣機？

Person B: 沒有，可是離洗衣服的地方不遠。

Person A: 我不喜歡做飯，附近有飯館兒嗎？

Person B: 有，旁邊有一家很地道的中國飯館兒。

Person A: 房租多少錢？

Person B: 每個月四百塊。

1 Would you rent this apartment?

_____

2 Explain your decision by commenting briefly on the following things:

air conditioning _____

size of bathroom _____

age of building _____

noise level _____

laundry facilities _____

restaurants _____

rent _____

Read the passage, then mark the statements true or false. **INTERPRETIVE**

在中国，学生高中毕业以后都得考试才能上大学。考试考得好，就上好一点儿的大学；考得不太好，就上一般的大学。如果考试考得很不好，就不能上大学。很多大学新生一进学校，就已经知道自己的专业是什么了，要是不喜欢，也可以换专业。但是换专业，还是得考试。

在中國，學生高中畢業以後都得考試才能上大學。考試考得好，就上好一點兒的大學；考得不太好，就上一般的大學。如果考試考得很不好，就不能上大學。很多大學新生一進學校，就已經知道自己的專業是什麼了，要是不喜歡，也可以換專業。但是換專業，還是得考試。

1 ____ High school graduates in China cannot enter college without first taking an exam.

2 ____ High school graduates who do not do well on the college exam all have to attend second-rate colleges.

3 ____ Chinese college students can easily switch majors.

D Read the passage, then draw a picture and mark the statements true or false. **INTERPRETIVE**

小高的新家有两层楼。楼上有三个房间。左边的房间是小高的书房。书房中间是一张很大的书桌，书桌后边是两个又高又大的书架。中间的房间是厕所。厕所的右边是小高的卧室，卧室中间放着一张床，床旁边摆着一个衣柜。楼下有客厅、餐厅、厨房和洗衣房。洗衣房在右边，里边有洗衣机和干衣机。洗衣房的旁边是餐厅和厨房，最左边是客厅。小高站在门外，看着自己的新家，非常高兴。

小高的新家有兩層樓。樓上有三個房間。左邊的房間是小高的書房。書房中間是一張很大的書桌，書桌後邊是兩個又高又大的書架。中間的房間是廁所。廁所的右邊是小高的臥室，臥室中間放著一張床，床旁邊擺著一個衣櫃。樓下有客廳、餐廳、廚房和洗衣房。洗衣房在右邊，裡邊有洗衣機和乾衣機。洗衣房的旁邊是餐廳和廚房，最左邊是客廳。小高站在門外，看著自己的新家，非常高興。

1 ___ 这个房子有五个房间。

  ___ 這個房子有五個房間。

2 ___ 小高不用花钱到外边洗衣服，可以在家洗。

  ___ 小高不用花錢到外邊洗衣服，可以在家洗。

3 ___ 要是小高的朋友来家里聊天儿、吃饭，他们应该到
      楼上去。

  ___ 要是小高的朋友來家裡聊天兒、吃飯，他們應該到
      樓上去。

这个商店卖不卖纸和笔？你怎么知道？

這個商店賣不賣紙和筆？你怎麼知道？

A Form a character by combining the given components as instructed. Then use that character to write a word, phrase, or short sentence.

1 左边一个"毛"，右边两个"火"，
  左邊一個"毛"，右邊兩個"火"，
  是 _____ 的 _____ 。

2 左边一个"木"，右边一个"东"，
  左邊一個"木"，右邊一個"東"，
  是 _____ 的 _____ 。

3 上边一个"口"，下边两个"口"，
  上邊一個"口"，下邊兩個"口"，
  是 _____ 的 _____ 。

4 外边一个"门"，里边一个"日"，
  外邊一個"門"，裡邊一個"日"，
  是 _____ 的 _____ 。

B Answer these questions based on your own circumstances. INTERPERSONAL

1 Q: 学校附近的饭馆儿，你比较喜欢哪一家？
     學校附近的飯館兒，你比較喜歡哪一家？

  A: _____

2 Q: 你觉得住校内比较省钱，还是住校外比较省钱？
     你覺得住校內比較省錢，還是住校外比較省錢？

  A: _____

3　Q: 学校里的哪一栋楼比较新？
　　　學校裡的哪一棟樓比較新？

　　A: _____

Complete these dialogues using 比较/比較, following the example below. INTERPERSONAL

Person A: 这个店的家具太贵了，我想看看别的店怎么样。

這個店的傢俱太貴了，我想看看別的店怎麼樣。

Person B: <u>这个店的家具虽然比较贵</u>，但是比别的店的都好得多。

<u>這個店的傢俱雖然比較貴</u>，但是比別的店的都好得多。

1　**Person A:** 我不想住校，宿舍房间太小了。

我不想住校，宿舍房間太小了。

　　Person B: _____，但是离教室近，上课很方便。

_____，但是離教室近，上課很方便。

2　**Person A:** 这台洗衣机太吵了，应该买一台新的。

這台洗衣機太吵了，應該買一台新的。

　　Person B: _____，但是还可以用。

_____，但是還可以用。

3　**Person A:** 你怎么带我来这家餐馆儿？你看他们的桌子椅子那么旧。

你怎麼帶我來這家餐館兒？你看他們的桌子椅子那麼舊。

　　Person B: _____，但是菜又好吃又便宜。

_____，但是菜又好吃又便宜。

D Rewrite these sentences using 得很, following the example below. **PRESENTATIONAL**

那家饭馆儿的菜非常地道。→ 那家饭馆儿的菜地道得很。
那家飯館兒的菜非常地道。→ 那家飯館兒的菜地道得很。

1 他住的那栋宿舍非常安静。
他住的那棟宿舍非常安靜。

_____

2 这个学校非常安全。
這個學校非常安全。

_____

3 那家商店非常远。
那家商店非常遠。

_____

E Complete these sentences using 恐怕/恐怕, following the example below. **INTERPERSONAL**

Q: 哎，你的房间怎么这么热？
哎，你的房間怎麼這麼熱？

A: 我也不知道，<u>恐怕是空调坏了</u>。
我也不知道，<u>恐怕是空調壞了</u>。

1 Q: 他明天能来吗？
他明天能來嗎？

A: 他这两天非常忙，_____。
他這兩天非常忙，_____。

2   Person A: 我刚下课，肚子饿得很。我想去学生餐厅吃晚
                饭。
                我剛下課，肚子餓得很。我想去學生餐廳吃晚
                飯。

    Person B: 可是现在已经快九点了。这么晚了，

                _____。

                可是現在已經快九點了。這麼晚了，

                _____。

3   Q: 你觉得我应该买几个书架？
       你覺得我應該買幾個書架？

    A: 你的房间不大，如果书架太多，_____，
       最好只买一个。
       你的房間不大，如果書架太多，_____，
       最好只買一個。

F   Rearrange these words into complete sentences. Pay attention to the Chinese word order.
        PRESENTATIONAL

1   书   一本   买了   我妹妹   很有意思的
    書   一本   買了   我妹妹   很有意思的

    _____

2   从北京   前天   我   是   来的   坐飞机
    從北京   前天   我   是   來的   坐飛機

    _____

3   六个月   两年前   工作了   他   在中国
    六個月   兩年前   工作了   他   在中國

    _____

4 一些　在那家饭馆儿　我们　昨天　很地道的　吃了　中国菜

  一些　在那家飯館兒　我們　昨天　很地道的　吃了　中國菜

_____

5 写　　中国字　　小王　　很快　　写得

  寫　　中國字　　小王　　很快　　寫得

_____

G Describe these scenes. Don't forget to mention what's in the background and, if applicable, what the person is wearing. Remember to use 着/著 in your description. PRESENTATIONAL

1

_____

_____

_____

_____

2
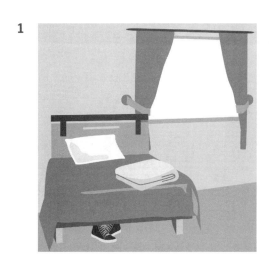

_____

_____

_____

_____

3

_____

_____

_____

_____

H Translate these dialogues into Chinese. PRESENTATIONAL

1 Q: Where is your roommate from?

_____

A: He's from New York.

_____

2 Person A: I'm starving.

_____

Person B: Then let's go eat.

_____

3 Q: Does the campus store sell furniture?

_____

A: No, campus stores generally don't sell furniture. They only sell daily necessities and stationery.

_____

_____

I Translate these sentences into Chinese. Pay attention to the Chinese word order, especially the position of time and place words. PRESENTATIONAL

1 I read a new book in the library yesterday afternoon.

_____

2 My brother drove from northern California to southern California last weekend to visit a friend.

_____

3 He was doing laundry on the second floor when his father called.

_____

4 Little Zhang is going to play basketball with his friends after class.

_____

J Translate these sentences into Chinese. Remember that the modifier/attributive always precedes the modified noun.

1 This is the restaurant that my roommate mentioned.

_____

2 The dorm where I used to live was very small and very old.

_____

3 The food that your mom made last night was extremely tasty.

_____

4 The bookstore we went to this morning also sells sportswear.

_____

K Translate these passages into Chinese using the grammar points and vocabulary items from this lesson. PRESENTATIONAL

1 Near campus there are a Chinese restaurant and a Japanese restaurant. The Japanese restaurant is rather expensive. The Chinese restaurant is much cheaper than the Japanese restaurant. Both restaurants are very close to campus. They're really convenient.

_____

_____

_____

2 This is Zhang Tianming's room. There is a bed in the middle of the room. On the bed, there is a blanket and a comforter. On the right side of the room is a wardrobe. However, the wardrobe is empty. There's a bookshelf on the left side of the room. There are some books on the shelf.

_____

_____

_____

3 I am moving into the dorms in a few days. The dorm is relatively new. My room is close to the bathroom. There are washers and dryers on my floor. It's really convenient to live there. However, I'm afraid it will be a bit noisy.

_____

_____

_____

L Describe your living quarters. Be sure to mention the location, the layout of your room, whether it is quiet for study and convenient for shopping, and finally, whether you like living there and why. PRESENTATIONAL

_____

_____

_____

_____

M Write a story in Chinese based on the four images below. Make sure that your story has a beginning, middle, and end, and that the transition from one picture to the next is smooth and logical. PRESENTATIONAL

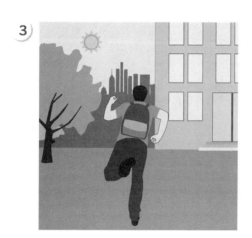

_____

_____

_____

_____

_____

在饭馆儿
在飯館兒
At a Restaurant

 Check off the following language functions as you learn how to:

[ ] Name several popular Chinese dishes and the four principal regional Chinese cuisines

[ ] Talk about what flavors you prefer

[ ] Specify seasonings you do and don't want in your food

[ ] Describe dietary restrictions and preferences

As you progress through the lesson, note other language functions you would like to learn.

_____

_____

_____

Audio

A Listen to the Lesson Text audio, then circle the most appropriate choice. **INTERPRETIVE**

1 **Why did Zhang Tianming want to go to a Chinese restaurant?**

   a   Ke Lin invited him out for a Chinese meal.

   b   He and his girlfriend wanted to have a Chinese meal.

   c   Ke Lin and his girlfriend wanted to go with him.

2 **Who went to the restaurant with Zhang Tianming?**

   a   Ke Lin and Lin Xuemei

   b   Lisha and Lin Xuemei

   c   Lisha, Ke Lin, and Lin Xuemei

3 **Who are more familiar with the menu of the restaurant?**

   a   Ke Lin and Lin Xuemei

   b   Ke Lin and Zhang Tianming

   c   Lisha and Lin Xuemei

4 **Which of the following did they NOT order?**

   a   rice

   b   dumplings

   c   soup

5 **Which Chinese cooking style(s) does Zhang Tianming prefer?**

   a   Shanghainese

   b   Sichuanese and Hunanese

   c   We do not know.

6 **What do they request?**

   a   four glasses of ice water, four pairs of chopsticks, and more than four paper napkins

   b   four glasses of ice water, two pairs of chopsticks, and some paper napkins

   c   four glasses of ice water, four pairs of chopsticks, and four paper napkins

7 **Lin Xuemei apologizes**

   a   to her friends for joking with the waiter.

   b   to the waiter for making a joke at his expense.

   c   to the waiter for making too many requests.

B Listen to the Workbook Dialogue audio, then mark these statements true or false. INTERPRETIVE

1 _____ The restaurant has been in business for almost a decade.

2 _____ The Zhang family moved from Guangdong to Shanghai many years ago.

3 _____ The restaurant's dishes are typically spicy and salty.

4 _____ The male speaker has never eaten at the restaurant.

C Based on the Workbook Dialogue audio, circle the most appropriate choice. INTERPRETIVE

1 Which of the following best describes the man's perception of Chinese cuisine?

   a   All Chinese restaurants season their food heavily.

   b   The major Chinese cooking styles are clearly distinct from one another.

   c   Sichuanese cuisine is the only authentic Chinese cuisine.

2 Which of the following best describes the woman's attitude toward Chinese restaurants?

   a   A good Chinese restaurant must be either Shanghainese or Cantonese, but not both.

   b   A good Chinese restaurant must serve good beef with Chinese broccoli.

   c   A good Chinese restaurant doesn't have to conform to a major cooking style.

D Listen to the Workbook Narrative 1 audio, then mark these statements true or false. INTERPRETIVE

1 _____ Little Chen is thinking of quitting his job as a waiter at the restaurant.

2 _____ Little Chen became a vegetarian recently.

3 _____ Little Chen only likes the restaurant's vegetable dishes.

E Listen to the Workbook Narrative 2 audio. Based on the audio, in what three ways do Chinese and Americans differ when it comes to eating out? Answer in English. INTERPRETIVE

1 _____

2 _____

3 _____

F Listen to the Workbook Narrative 3 audio, then circle the dishes from the menu that suit Little Zhang's tastes. **INTERPRETIVE**

凉拌黄瓜/涼拌黃瓜   菠菜豆腐汤/菠菜豆腐湯

家常豆腐   米饭/米飯

清蒸鱼/清蒸魚   可乐/可樂

糖醋鱼/糖醋魚   冰茶/冰茶

红烧鸡/紅燒雞   冰咖啡

芥兰牛肉/芥蘭牛肉   热茶/熱茶

酸辣汤/酸辣湯   热咖啡/熱咖啡

小白菜汤/小白菜湯

G ___ Listen to the Workbook Listening Rejoinder audio. After hearing the first speaker, select the best response from the four choices given by the second speaker. Indicate the letter of your choice. **INTERPRETIVE**

II. Pinyin and Tone

A Compare the pronunciations of the underlined characters in the two words or phrases given. Provide their finals in *pinyin*.

考<u>虑</u>/考<u>慮</u> _____   马<u>路</u>/馬<u>路</u> _____

B Compare the tones of the underlined characters in the two words or phrases given. Indicate the tones with 1 (first tone), 2 (second tone), 3 (third tone), 4 (fourth tone), or 0 (neutral tone).

<u>每</u>天 _____   林雪<u>梅</u> _____

III. Speaking

A Practice asking and answering these questions. INTERPERSONAL

1 你吃过中国菜吗？学校附近有没有中国饭馆儿？

你吃過中國菜嗎？學校附近有沒有中國飯館兒？

2 你吃素吗？

你吃素嗎？

3 你先喝汤再吃菜，还是先吃菜再喝汤？还是一边吃菜、一边喝汤？

你先喝湯再吃菜，還是先吃菜再喝湯？還是一邊吃菜、一邊喝湯？

4 你会用筷子吗？

你會用筷子嗎？

B Practice speaking with these prompts. INTERPERSONAL

1 你喜欢吃什么口味的菜？咸的？甜的？辣的？还是清淡的？

你喜歡吃什麼口味的菜？鹹的？甜的？辣的？還是清淡的？

2 如果在中国饭馆儿点菜，你会点什么菜？

如果在中國飯館兒點菜，你會點什麼菜？

C In pairs, role-play two friends making plans to eat out at a Chinese restaurant. In Chinese, extend your partner an invitation, and decide on a place, date, and time. Ask about each other's favorite dishes. Discuss your dietary preferences or restrictions and decide which dishes to order based on both people's tastes. INTERPERSONAL

A Write the characters, *pinyin*, and English equivalent of each new word formed. Guess the meaning, then use a dictionary to confirm.

1 "名字"的"名"+"菜单"的"单"

"名字"的"名"+"菜單"的"單"

→ 名 + 单/單→ _____ _____ _____

2 "鸡"+"蛋糕"的"蛋"

"雞"+"蛋糕"的"蛋"

→ 鸡/雞 + 蛋→ _____ _____ _____

3 "清蒸鱼"的"鱼"+"干衣机"的"干"

"清蒸魚"的"魚"+"乾衣機"的"乾"

→ 鱼/魚 + 干/乾→ _____ _____ _____

4 "汽车"的"汽"+"油"

"汽車"的"汽"+"油"

→ 汽 + 油→ _____ _____ _____

5 "出去"的"出"+"门口"的"口"

"出去"的"出"+"門口"的"口"

→ 出 + 口→ _____ _____ _____

B Draw lines to connect each cuisine with its signature flavor. INTERPRETIVE

四川菜/四川菜   清淡

广东菜/廣東菜   甜

上海菜/上海菜   辣

C Which of these dishes do you think are vegetarian? Use check marks to indicate your answers.
INTERPRETIVE

Dishes	Yes	No	Sometimes
凉拌黄瓜/涼拌黃瓜			
家常豆腐			
红烧牛肉/紅燒牛肉			
芥兰牛肉/芥蘭牛肉			
清蒸鱼/清蒸魚			
糖醋鱼/糖醋魚			
酸辣汤/酸辣湯			
菠菜豆腐汤/菠菜豆腐湯			

D Read the passage, then answer the question in Chinese. INTERPERSONAL

有的人觉得应该想吃什么就吃什么，不要怕油多。有的人觉得菜越清淡越好，应该多吃青菜，少吃肉，特别是少吃牛肉。做菜的时候，要少放油，少放盐。你觉得呢？

有的人覺得應該想吃什麼就吃什麼，不要怕油多。有的人覺得菜越清淡越好，應該多吃青菜，少吃肉，特別是少吃牛肉。做菜的時候，要少放油，少放鹽。你覺得呢？

小柯常到学校附近的一家中国饭馆儿吃饭。那家饭馆儿的菜又便宜又地道，他是那儿的常客，服务员都认识他。小柯今天又去那儿吃午饭。但是他一进门，就觉得跟以前不一样了。这家饭馆儿的菜以前非常清淡，可是今天油怎么这么多？还有，今天的服务员他一个都不认识。菜单上的菜也比以前贵多了。除了这些以外，他点的菜里还放了很多味精。他想下次再也不到这家饭馆儿来吃饭了。

小柯常到學校附近的一家中國飯館兒吃飯。那家飯館兒的菜又便宜又地道，他是那兒的常客，服務員都認識他。小柯今天又去那兒吃午飯。但是他一進門，就覺得跟以前不一樣了。這家飯館兒的菜以前非常清淡，可是今天油怎麼這麼多？還有，今天的服務員他一個都不認識。菜單上的菜也比以前貴多了。除了這些以外，他點的菜裡還放了很多味精。他想下次再也不到這家飯館兒來吃飯了。

1 **What previously attracted Little Ke to the restaurant?**

  a the authentic dishes and reasonable prices

  b the welcoming attitude of the wait staff

  c both of the above

2 **What changes did Little Ke notice on this visit?**

  a new waitstaff, higher prices, and the use of MSG and more oil

  b new waitstaff, higher prices, and fewer customers

  c the use of MSG and more oil, new waitstaff, and more customers

F Based on the passage in (E), mark these statements true or false. **INTERPRETIVE**

1 _____ Little Ke didn't eat on this visit to the restaurant.

2 _____ Little Ke will not eat there again.

Read the passage, then mark the statements true or false. Note: 吃醋 can mean "to eat vinegar" or "to be jealous." **INTERPRETIVE**

今天是太太的生日，李先生很早就从公司回家，想给太太做一个红烧鱼。鱼做好了，李先生觉得味道太淡。他加了一点儿盐，还是太淡，又加了一点儿盐，还是太淡。李先生觉得不对，原来自己把糖当成盐了。他就在菜里放了一些醋，把红烧鱼做成了糖醋鱼。太太笑着说："我不是爱吃醋的女人。"李先生说："多吃醋对身体有好处！"

今天是太太的生日，李先生很早就從公司回家，想給太太做一個紅燒魚。魚做好了，李先生覺得味道太淡。他加了一點兒鹽，還是太淡，又加了一點兒鹽，還是太淡。李先生覺得不對，原來自己把糖當成鹽了。他就在菜裡放了一些醋，把紅燒魚做成了糖醋魚。太太笑著說："我不是愛吃醋的女人。"李先生說："多吃醋對身體有好處！"

1 ____ Mr. Li didn't go to work today.

2 ____ Mr. Li put a lot of salt in the fish.

3 ____ Vinegar is one of the essential ingredients in Mr. Li's original fish recipe.

4 ____ Mr. Li put a lot of vinegar in the fish because Mrs. Li likes vinegar.

5 ____ Mrs. Li does not see herself as a jealous woman.

H Read the passage, then answer the question in the passage in English. **INTERPRETIVE**

这是我从我的中文老师那儿听来的：

今天是小明的生日，爸爸妈妈带他到饭馆儿吃饭。爸爸说他们要去的饭馆儿是小朋友最喜欢的。但是到了饭馆儿门前，小明看见饭馆儿的名字，就哭着说："我不进去！"妈妈说："你为什么不进去呀？"小明说："我怕！"

爸爸看到饭馆儿的名字是"友朋小吃"，就笑了起来。你们知道小明为什么怕，爸爸为什么笑吗？

這是我從我的中文老師那兒聽來的：

今天是小明的生日，爸爸媽媽帶他到飯館兒吃飯。爸爸說他們要去的飯館兒是小朋友最喜歡的。但是到了飯館兒門前，小明看見飯館兒的名字，就哭著說：" 我不進去！" 媽媽說：" 你為什麼不進去呀？" 小明說：" 我怕！"

爸爸看到飯館兒的名字是 " 友朋小吃 "，就笑了起來。你們知道小明為什麼怕，爸爸為什麼笑嗎？

Hint: The sign can be read as an anagram. Ask your teacher to explain how shop signs, placards, and newspaper headlines were traditionally inscribed in China.

I   This is a set menu for a multi-course meal. Try your best to tell your friends who don't read Chinese what's on the menu. INTERPRETIVE

★ 前菜
★ 沙拉
★ 汤
★ 主餐
★ 甜点
★ 饮料

★ 前菜
★ 沙拉
★ 湯
★ 主餐
★ 甜點
★ 飲料

J This is an excerpt from a cookbook. Answer in English what the dish is and if it is vegetarian.

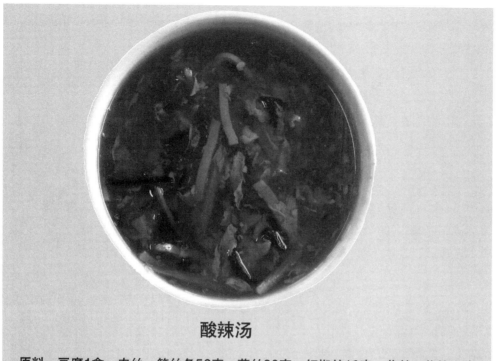

酸辣汤

原料：豆腐1盒，肉丝，笋丝各50克，菇丝30克，红椒丝10克，葱丝、姜丝、油、胡椒粉、湿淀粉各适量，鸡蛋1只，A: 酱油、味粉、醋各适量。

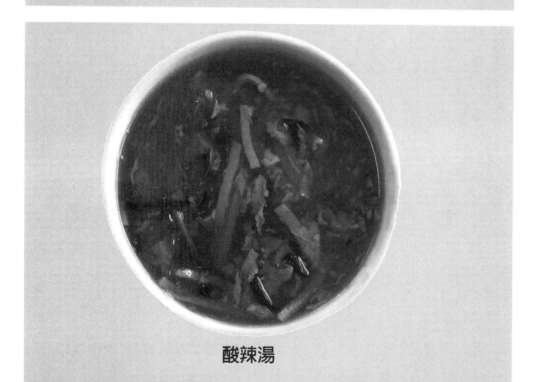

酸辣湯

原料：豆腐1盒，肉絲，筍絲各50克，菇絲30克，紅椒絲10克，蔥絲、薑絲、油、胡椒粉、濕澱粉各適量，雞蛋1只，A: 醬油、味粉、醋各適量。

A Form a character by combining the given components as instructed. Then use that character to write a word, phrase, or short sentence.

1 左边一个"鱼"，右边一个"羊"，

左邊一個"魚"，右邊一個"羊"，

是 ＿＿＿＿＿＿ 的 ＿＿＿。

2 左边三点水，右边两个"火"，

左邊三點水，右邊兩個"火"，

是 ＿＿＿＿＿＿ 的 ＿＿＿。

3 左边三点水，右边一个"自由"的"由"，

左邊三點水，右邊一個"自由"的"由"，

是 ＿＿＿＿＿＿ 的 ＿＿＿。

4 左边一个"木"，右边一个"每天"的"每"，

左邊一個"木"，右邊一個"每天"的"每"，

是 ＿＿＿＿＿＿ 的 ＿＿＿。

B Answer these questions using the underlined phrases as the topics, following the example below.

INTERPERSONAL

Q: 学校附近有很多饭馆儿，还有<u>一家中国餐馆儿</u>，不知道那儿的菜怎么样？

学校附近有很多飯館兒，還有<u>一家中國餐館兒</u>，不知道那兒的菜怎麼樣？

A: 那家餐馆儿我去过，菜做得很地道。

那家餐館兒我去過，菜做得很地道。

1 Q: 张天明认识<u>柯林的女朋友</u>吗？
　　张天明認識<u>柯林的女朋友</u>嗎？

　　A: _____

2 Q: 张天明已经适应<u>宿舍的生活</u>了吗？
　　張天明已經適應<u>宿舍的生活</u>了嗎？

　　A: _____

3 Q: 你吃过<u>四川菜</u>吗？味道怎么样？
　　你吃過<u>四川菜</u>嗎？味道怎麼樣？

　　A: _____

4 Q: 你会写<u>第二课的生词</u>吗？
　　你會寫<u>第二課的生詞</u>嗎？

　　A: _____

C Paraphrase these sentences using 一⋯就⋯. PRESENTATIONAL

1 这课的语法很容易，老师刚讲完，我就懂了。
　这課的語法很容易，老師剛講完，我就懂了。

　_____

2 他很聪明，什么字，你教他，他很快就会了。
　他很聰明，什麼字，你教他，他很快就會了。

　_____

3 那个地方很近，很快就走到了。
　那個地方很近，很快就走到了。

　_____

D | Rewrite these sentences using 又⋯又⋯. Follow the example below. <u>PRESENTATIONAL</u>

那栋宿舍很新，也很漂亮。 → 那栋宿舍又新又漂亮。
那棟宿舍很新，也很漂亮。 → 那棟宿舍又新又漂亮。

1 我妈妈做的牛肉很嫩，而且很香。
　我媽媽做的牛肉很嫩，而且很香。

　→ _____ 。

2 那家饭馆儿的菜不但很辣，而且很咸。
　那家飯館兒的菜不但很辣，而且很鹹。

　→ _____ 。

3 那家商店卖的有机青菜、有机水果非常新鲜，而且很好吃。
　那家商店賣的有機青菜、有機水果非常新鮮，而且很好吃 。

　→ _____ 。

E | Based on your own circumstances or opinion, answer these questions using 这就要看⋯了/這就要看⋯了. <u>INTERPERSONAL</u>

1 Q: 你下个学期还要学中文吗？
　　你下個學期還要學中文嗎？

　A: _____ 。

2 Q: 你这个周末打算做什么？
　　你這個週末打算做什麼？

　A: _____ 。

3 Q: 你觉得大学新生应该住校内还是住校外？
　　你覺得大學新生應該住校內還是住校外？

　A: _____ 。

F Based on the information given, describe what the characters in the textbook pariularly like or dislike, using 特别是/特別是, following the example below. PRESENTATIONAL

张天明喜欢吃肉，特别是鸡。

張天明喜歡吃肉，特別是雞。

1

_____

2

_____

3

_____

　　我问同学他们觉得附近哪一家餐馆儿＿＿＿菜做＿＿＿最好吃。他们告诉我学校南边那家中国饭馆儿＿＿＿菜最好。听说，那家餐馆儿上菜上＿＿＿快，菜也做＿＿＿很地道。地方又大又安静。大家都喜欢在那儿慢慢儿＿＿＿吃，边吃饭，边聊天儿。

　　我問同學他們覺得附近哪一家餐館兒＿＿＿菜做＿＿＿最好吃。他們告訴我學校南邊那家中國飯館兒＿＿＿菜最好。聽說，那家餐館兒上菜上＿＿＿快，菜也做＿＿＿很地道。地方又大又安靜。大家都喜歡在那兒慢慢兒＿＿＿吃，邊吃飯，邊聊天兒。

H Fill in the blanks with the words and phrases provided. **INTERPRETIVE**

要不然　　又…又…　　这就要看　　非常　　比较　　特别是

　　我觉得这家餐馆儿的菜做得＿＿＿＿好，＿＿＿＿他们的清蒸鱼，＿＿＿＿新鲜＿＿＿＿好吃。但是有的人觉得他们的菜太清淡。所以如果你要问这家餐馆儿的菜好不好，＿＿＿＿你的口味了。我自己吃得＿＿＿＿清淡，＿＿＿＿，我就不会说这家餐馆儿的菜好吃了。

要不然　　又…又…　　這就要看　　非常　　比較　　特別是

　　我覺得這家餐館兒的菜做得＿＿＿＿好，＿＿＿＿他們的清蒸魚，＿＿＿＿新鮮＿＿＿＿好吃。但是有的人覺得他們的菜太清淡。所以如果你要問這家餐館兒的菜好不好，＿＿＿＿你的口味了。我自己吃得＿＿＿＿清淡，＿＿＿＿，我就不會說這家餐館兒的菜好吃了。

Translate these sentences into Chinese. **PRESENTATIONAL**

1 I finished reading the book I bought yesterday. (topic-comment)

_____

2 Your younger sister is very pretty. （长得/長得）

_____

3 The steamed fish tastes excellent.

_____

4 The beef and broccoli at this restaurant is superb. The beef is tender and smells wonderful.
（又⋯又⋯）

_____

5 Could I trouble you not to put any MSG in the food?

_____

_____

J Translate these passages into Chinese. **PRESENTATIONAL**

1 Ke Lin and Zhang Tianming went out to eat last night. Ke Lin drove very fast, so they got to Chinatown very quickly. The dishes that they ordered were all delicious. As soon as they finished eating, they went back to school. While driving, they talked and laughed. They were very happy.

_____

_____

_____

2 I hadn't had Chinese food for three weeks. I was thinking about having some authentic Chinese food in Chinatown. As it happened, my friend Little Lin also wanted to have some Chinese food. But neither of us had a car. It took us an hour to walk there. We ordered three dishes. They smelled good and tasted great. We both felt that we should have ordered more.

_____

_____

_____

_____

K Write a restaurant review in Chinese. In your review, comment on the decor of the restaurant, the service, the prices, and your favorite dishes. PRESENTATIONAL

_____

_____

_____

L Write a story in Chinese based on the four images below. Make sure that your story has a beginning, middle, and end, and that the transition from one picture to the next is smooth and logical. PRESENTATIONAL

CHINESE RESTAURANT

Carryout Box: 15 cents

_____

_____

_____

_____

买东西
買東西
Shopping

 Check off the following language functions as you learn how to:

[ ] Name basic clothing, bedding, and bath items

[ ] Describe shopping preferences and criteria

[ ] Present opinions using rhetorical statements

As you progress through the lesson, note other language functions you would like to learn.

_____

_____

_____

I. Listening Comprehension

A Listen to the Lesson Text audio, then mark these statements true or false. INTERPRETIVE

1 _____ Zhang Tianming doesn't like the clothes that his mother bought for him.

2 _____ Zhang Tianming believes that name-brand clothes are superior in quality.

3 _____ For Ke Lin, the most important criterion for buying clothes is price.

4 _____ Lisha agrees with Ke Lin's clothes-shopping philosophy.

B Listen to the Workbook Dialogue audio, then mark these statements true or false. INTERPRETIVE

1 _____ The woman urges the man not to worry about her wardrobe.

2 _____ The man and woman went shopping together last weekend.

3 _____ The woman has not bought many clothes recently because she wants to save money.

4 _____ The woman thinks her clothes are not only all name-brand, but also fashionable.

5 _____ It is difficult for the woman to buy clothes because she is too picky about prices.

C Listen to the Workbook Narrative 1 audio, then mark these statements true or false. INTERPRETIVE

1 _____ In the past, most Chinese paid for their purchases in cash.

2 _____ As in most of the U.S., there is sales tax in China.

3 _____ More and more shoppers in China use credit cards to pay.

D Listen to the Workbook Narrative 2 audio, then mark these statements true or false. INTERPRETIVE

1 _____ Little Lin buys only stylish and expensive clothes.

2 _____ Little Wang likes to wear name-brand clothes.

3 _____ As good friends, Little Lin and Little Wang often go shopping for clothes together.

E Listen to the Workbook Narrative 3 audio, then circle the most appropriate choice. INTERPRETIVE

1 Which of the following is part of the name of the shopping center?

a Huanying

b Dada

c Dongxi

2 How many floors are there?

a two

b three

c four

3 If you wanted to buy shoes, which floor would you go to?

    a   second

    b   third

    c   fourth

4 What is the discount for the New Year sale?

    a   twenty-five percent off

    b   fifty percent off

    c   seventy-five percent off

5 In addition to the sale, what extra incentive is there for customers?

    a   a pair of shoes

    b   a coffee mug

    c   a shopping bag

F Listen to the Workbook Narrative 4 audio, then circle the most appropriate choice. **INTERPRETIVE**

1 What does the hotel NOT provide to guests?

    a   towels

    b   pajamas

    c   toothpaste

2 Guests can pay their bills

    a   with a credit card.

    b   in cash.

    c   in cash or with a credit card.

3 What is the disadvantage of staying at this hotel?

    a   There is no air conditioning.

    b   There is no Internet.

    c   There is a high hotel tax.

4 If the room rate is $100 per night, how much does it cost to stay for one night including tax?

    a $110

    b $115

    c $120

G ____ Listen to the Workbook Listening Rejoinder audio. After hearing the first speaker, select the best response from the four choices given by the second speaker. Indicate the letter of your choice. **INTERPRETIVE**

A Compare the pronunciations of the underlined characters in the two words/phrases given. Provide their initials in *pinyin*.

需要 _____   舒服 _____

B Compare the tones of the underlined characters in the two words/phrases given. Indicate the tones with 1 (first tone), 2 (second tone), 3 (third tone), 4 (fourth tone), or 0 (neutral tone).

买东西/買東西 _____   卖东西/賣東西 _____

III. Speaking

A Practice asking and answering these questions. INTERPERSONAL

1 你一般多久买一次衣服？
　你一般多久買一次衣服？

2 你现在身上穿的衣服是什么颜色的？
　你現在身上穿的衣服是什麼顏色的？

3 你买衣服的标准是什么？
　你買衣服的標準是什麼？

4 一般来说，买完东西的时候，你付现金还是用信用卡？
　一般來說，買完東西的時候，你付現金還是用信用卡？

5 你现在住的州买衣服需要付税吗？
　你現在住的州買衣服需要付稅嗎？

B Practice speaking with these prompts. PRESENTATIONAL

1 你跟你的朋友一起去买东西，他看到什么都想买，你怎么做能让他少买一些？

你跟你的朋友一起去買東西，他看到什麼都想買，你怎麼做能讓他少買一些？

2 请你说说你对名牌衣服的看法。你买衣服一定要买名牌的吗？为什么？

請你說說你對名牌衣服的看法。你買衣服一定要買名牌的嗎？為什麼？

3 You are a salesperson and have to sell this T-shirt. Talk to a potential customer about the T-shirt based on the information on the clothing label and tag, and try to convince the customer that the T-shirt's style, color, material, and price are wonderful and ideal for him/her.

DKNY

Original: $40

Now: $20

Made in China

100% cotton

Machine wash

Tumble dry

IV. Reading Comprehension

A Complete this section by writing the characters, *pinyin*, and English equivalent of each new word formed. Guess the meaning, then use a dictionary to confirm.

1 "长短"的"短"+"牛仔裤"的"裤"

"長短"的"短"+"牛仔褲"的"褲"

→ 短 + 裤/褲→ _____ _____ _____

2 "校内"的"内"+"衣服"的"衣"

"校內"的"內"+"衣服"的"衣"

→ 内/內 ＋ 衣→ _____ _____ _____

3 "汽车"的"车"+"牌子"的"牌"

"汽車"的"車"+"牌子"的"牌"

→ 车/車 ＋ 牌→ _____ _____ _____

4 "吃药"的"药"+"牙膏"的"膏"

"吃藥"的"藥"+"牙膏"的"膏"

→ 药/藥 ＋ 膏→ _____ _____ _____

5 "牙膏"的"牙"+"刷卡"的"刷"

"牙膏"的"牙"+"刷卡"的"刷"

→ 牙 ＋ 刷→ _____ _____ _____

B Read the passage, then mark the statements true or false. INTERPRETIVE

　　柯林买衣服只要样子、颜色、大小、长短合适就行，不在乎是不是名牌。他的女朋友林雪梅觉得名牌的衣服质量更好，穿起来也更舒服。上个周末柯林买了一件衬衫，是雪梅最不喜欢的黄色，然后穿着去见她。雪梅一见柯林就叫起来："你怎么买了一件这么难看的衣服？"柯林笑着说："这是名牌的！你不喜欢吗？"

　　柯林買衣服只要樣子、顏色、大小、長短合適就行，不在乎是不是名牌。他的女朋友林雪梅覺得名牌的衣服質量更好，穿起來也更舒服。上個週末柯林買了一件襯衫，是雪梅最不喜歡的黃色，然後穿著去見她。雪梅一見柯林就叫起來："你怎麼買了一件這麼難看的衣服？"柯林笑著說："這是名牌的！你不喜歡嗎？"

1 ____ Ke Lin does not care about name-brand clothes.

2 ____ For Lin Xuemei, a good brand means good quality.

3 ____ Last weekend, Ke Lin and Lin Xuemei went shopping together.

4 ____ Ke Lin tried to make the point that name-brand clothes are not necessarily good.

C Read the passage and check the boxes in the table based on the information given and your own circumstances. Then answer the question in Chinese. **INTERPRETIVE & INTERPERSONAL**

　　小张买东西的标准是：只要是名牌的，无论样子好不好，价钱贵不贵，他都要买。小林买东西跟小张不一样，很在乎质量，而且要价钱便宜。他们两个一起出去买衣服的时候，小张觉得小林只想省钱，不在乎牌子；小林觉得小张只想穿名牌，不在乎衣服样子合适不合适。所以他们常常出去的时候很高兴，回来的时候很不高兴。

　　你呢？你会跟小张还是小林一起去买东西？为什么？

　　小張買東西的標準是：只要是名牌的，無論樣子好不好，價錢貴不貴，他都要買。小林買東西跟小張不一樣，很在乎質量，而且要價錢便宜。他們兩個一起出去買衣服的時候，小張覺得小林只想省錢，不在乎牌子；小林覺得小張只想穿名牌，不在乎衣服樣子合適不合適。所以他們常常出去的時候很高興，回來的時候很不高興。

　　你呢？你會跟小張還是小林一起去買東西？為什麼？

	Brand Name	Price	Style	Quality
Little Zhang	☐	☐	☐	☐
Little Lin	☐	☐	☐	☐
You	☐	☐	☐	☐

Your answer: _____

_____

D State in English what this sign says. INTERPRETIVE

E Read this advertisement for a department store sale, then answer the questions in English. INTERPRETIVE

1 Which department is offering a forty-percent discount?

2 Is every item in that department forty percent off? How do you know?

3 Will customers shopping on Friday get the discount?

F Upscale boutiques and department stores are quite commonplace in cities across Mainland China. Skim through this advertisement from a Shanghai evening paper and complete the following tasks.

INTERPRETIVE

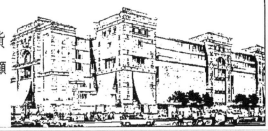

1 Circle the Chinese name of the store.

2 Circle the address of the store.

3 Circle the description that is used to convince the Chinese customer of the prestige of the store.

A Form a character by combining the given components as instructed. Then use that character to write a word, phrase, or short sentence.

1 左边一个人字旁，右边一个"子"，

左邊一個人字旁，右邊一個"子"，

是 _____ 的 ____。

2 上边一个"雨"，下边一个"而且"的"而"，

上邊一個"雨"，下邊一個"而且"的"而"，

是 _____ 的 ____。

3 上边一个"高"，下边一个"月"，

上邊一個"高"，下邊一個"月"，

是 _____ 的 ____。

4 左边一个"米"，右边一个"分钟"的"分"，

左邊一個"米"，右邊一個"分鐘"的"分"，

是 _____ 的 ____。

B Answer the questions in Chinese. **INTERPERSONAL**

1 Q: 今天是几月几号，星期几?

今天是幾月幾號，星期幾？

A: _____

2 Q: 这个学期开学多久了?

這個學期開學多久了？

A: _____

3 Q: 你一个星期上几次中文课？什么时候上？
　　你一個星期上幾次中文課？什麼時候上？

　　A: _____

4 Q: 你昨天做功课做了多长时间？
　　你昨天做功課做了多長時間？

　　A: _____

5 Q: 你多长时间没听录音了？
　　你多長時間沒聽錄音了？

　　A: _____

6 Q: 你多久洗一次衣服？
　　你多久洗一次衣服？

　　A: _____

7 Q: 从你住的地方开车到购物中心要开多长时间？
　　從你住的地方開車到購物中心要開多長時間？

　　A: _____

C　Complete these sentences using ⋯什么的/⋯什麼的, following the example below.
　　PRESENTATIONAL

这个购物中心真大，衣服、日用品什么的，你都能买到。
這個購物中心真大，衣服、日用品什麼的，你都能買到。

1　这家中国饭馆儿的菜很好吃，_____，都很地道。

　　這家中國飯館兒的菜很好吃，_____，都很地道。

2 他买衣服很花时间，＿＿＿＿＿＿＿＿＿＿，他都得看很
久。

他買衣服很花時間，＿＿＿＿＿＿＿＿＿＿，他都得看很
久。

3 跟他一起租房子真不容易，＿＿＿＿＿＿＿＿＿，他都要
问清楚。

跟他一起租房子真不容易，＿＿＿＿＿＿＿＿＿，他都要
問清楚。

D Rewrite these sentences using 无论⋯都⋯／無論⋯都⋯, following the example below.
PRESENTATIONAL

这两天他不太舒服，清蒸鱼、芥兰牛肉、菠菜豆腐什么
的，他都不想吃。

這兩天他不太舒服，清蒸魚、芥蘭牛肉、菠菜豆腐什麼
的，他都不想吃。

→ 这两天他不太舒服，无论什么菜，他都不想吃。

→ 這兩天他不太舒服，無論什麼菜，他都不想吃。

1 那个宿舍早上吵，中午吵，下午吵，晚上也吵。
那個宿舍早上吵，中午吵，下午吵，晚上也吵。

＿＿＿＿＿＿＿＿＿＿＿＿＿＿＿＿＿＿＿＿＿＿＿＿＿＿

2 这个城市的税很重。买吃的要付税，买穿的要付税，买
用的也要付税。

這個城市的稅很重。買吃的要付稅，買穿的要付稅，買
用的也要付稅。

＿＿＿＿＿＿＿＿＿＿＿＿＿＿＿＿＿＿＿＿＿＿＿＿＿＿

3 附近新开的购物中心非常大。吃的、穿的、用的、玩儿的，都能买到。

附近新開的購物中心非常大。吃的、穿的、用的、玩兒的，都能買到。

E Complete these sentences using 要不然, following the example below. **PRESENTATIONAL**

租房子最好租带家具的，<u>要不然得花很多钱买家具</u>。

租房子最好租帶傢俱的，<u>要不然得花很多錢買傢俱</u>。

1 学中文最好天天听录音，＿＿＿＿＿＿＿＿＿＿＿＿。

學中文最好天天聽錄音，＿＿＿＿＿＿＿＿＿＿＿＿。

2 在中国饭馆儿点菜，如果你不能吃比较咸的菜，就得告诉服务员少放点儿盐，＿＿＿＿＿＿＿＿＿＿。

在中國飯館兒點菜，如果你不能吃比較鹹的菜，就得告訴服務員少放點兒鹽，＿＿＿＿＿＿＿＿＿＿。

3 租房子最好不要租大马路旁边的，＿＿＿＿＿＿＿＿。

租房子最好不要租大馬路旁邊的，＿＿＿＿＿＿＿＿。

F You disagree with your friend on many issues, but you are always tactful. You always acknowledge that there might be some validity in your friend's view before stating your own opinion. Complete these sentences using the "adjective/verb + 是 + adjective/verb, 可是…" pattern, following the example below. **INTERPERSONAL**

Person A: 你为什么不喜欢去那家餐馆儿吃饭？他们的菜做得很地道。

你為什麼不喜歡去那家餐館兒吃飯？他們的菜做得很地道。

Person B: 他们的菜<u>地道是地道</u>，<u>可是</u>有点儿咸。

他們的菜<u>地道是地道</u>，<u>可是</u>有點兒鹹。

1 Person A: 中文不容易。
　　　　　　中文不容易。

　　Person B: ＿＿＿＿＿＿＿＿＿＿，＿＿＿＿＿＿＿＿＿＿。

2 Q: 住在校内很好，你为什么要搬出去?
　　住在校內很好，你為什麼要搬出去？

　　A: ＿＿＿＿＿＿＿＿＿＿，＿＿＿＿＿＿＿＿＿＿。

3 Q: 这栋楼那么旧，你为什么不搬到别的地方去?
　　這棟樓那麼舊，你為什麼不搬到別的地方去？

　　A: ＿＿＿＿＿＿＿＿＿＿，＿＿＿＿＿＿＿＿＿＿。

4 Q: 这条裤子你穿着很好看，为什么不买?
　　這條褲子你穿著很好看，為什麼不買？

　　A: ＿＿＿＿＿＿＿＿＿＿，＿＿＿＿＿＿＿＿＿＿。

G Complete these sentences using 非···不可···, following the example below. **PRESENTATIONAL**

天气又闷又热，<u>非下雨不可</u>，你别去打球了。
天氣又悶又熱，<u>非下雨不可</u>，你別去打球了。

1 今天我母亲过生日，晚上的生日晚会我 ＿＿＿＿＿＿＿。
　今天我母親過生日，晚上的生日晚會我 ＿＿＿＿＿＿＿。

2 他每次出去吃饭，＿＿＿＿＿＿＿，别的菜他都不喜欢吃。
　他每次出去吃飯，＿＿＿＿＿＿＿，別的菜他都不喜歡吃。

3 你天天吃那么多肉，又那么喜欢吃糖，＿＿＿＿＿＿＿。

你天天吃那麼多肉，又那麼喜歡吃糖，＿＿＿＿＿＿＿。

4 今天很冷，你穿得那么少，＿＿＿＿＿＿＿。

今天很冷，你穿得那麼少，＿＿＿＿＿＿＿。

H Translate this passage into English. **INTERPRETIVE**

　　小李只有在打折的时候才买衣服，一听说哪家商店打折，就非去买不可。我说："打折的东西便宜是便宜，但是质量也差一些。"小李说："衣服便宜可以多买几件，质量差一点儿没关系，穿坏了可以再买新的呀。"

　　小李只有在打折的時候才買衣服，一聽說哪家商店打折，就非去買不可。我說："打折的東西便宜是便宜，但是質量也差一些。"小李說："衣服便宜可以多買幾件，質量差一點兒沒關係，穿壞了可以再買新的呀。"

_____

_____

_____

_____

Translate these sentences into Chinese. **PRESENTATIONAL**

1 **Zhang Tianming doesn't have a car. He has to take the bus wherever he wants to go.**
   (无论···都··· / 無論···都···)

   _____

2 **They had dinner at a restaurant in Chinatown. The dishes that they ordered—Chinese broccoli, steamed fish, and so on—were all very delicious.**
   (···什么的 / ···什麼的)

   _____

   _____

3 **Person A:**   I feel that living on campus is better. It's very convenient.

   _____

   Person B: Living on campus is convenient, but it's too expensive.
   (adjective 是 adjective, 可是···)

   _____

4 **Person A:**   No matter what I buy, I always buy what's cheapest.

   _____

   Person B: Don't you care about quality?

   _____

5 **I won't buy this pair of shoes for my son. He wears nothing but name-brand shoes.**
   (非···不可···)

   _____

6 **Zhang Tianming wanted to buy a tracksuit, but he left his credit card in his dorm. He told the salesperson he would buy the tracksuit next week.**

   _____

   _____

Translate these sentences into Chinese. Pay special attention to the position of the time phrases.

1 Person A: For how long has your teacher been teaching Chinese?

_____

   Person B: My teacher has been teaching Chinese for five years.

_____

2 Person A: How long have you not had any Chinese food?

_____

   Person B: I haven't had any Chinese food for two weeks.

_____

3 Person A: How often do you do laundry?

_____

   Person B: I do laundry once a week.

_____

4 Person A: How many hours did your roommate sleep last night?

_____

   Person B: My roommate slept for three hours last night.

_____

5 Person A: How long do you work at the university bookstore every day?

_____

   Person B: I work for two hours at the university bookstore every day.

_____

6 **The doctor said that you have to drink water ten times a day.**

_____

7 Little Zhang sends his parents a WeChat message every two or three days.

_____

8 He moved three times last year.

_____

9 My brother hasn't bought any jeans for two years.

_____

10 He lived in the dorm for six months and moved off campus last week.

_____

K Translate these sentences into Chinese. **PRESENTATIONAL**

Person A: Is this set of clothes one-hundred-percent cotton? If it's not one-hundred-percent cotton, I'll be allergic to it.

_____

Person B: Yes, it's one-hundred-percent cotton. Both the color and quality of the clothes are very good. （无论···还是···/無論···還是···）

_____

Person A: I didn't bring cash. Can I use my credit card?

_____

Person B: I'm sorry. You can't use your card here. Why don't you come again tomorrow?

_____

L Translate this passage into Chinese. PRESENTATIONAL

Little Zhang came to the United States from China in March last year. He has been living in New York state for more than a year, and hasn't had any authentic Chinese food for six months. Before he came to the United States, he heard that it was very convenient to live in the United States. But now that he is in the United States, he doesn't think so. Since he doesn't have a car, he has to ask friends for help wherever he goes. He misses his parents very much and plans to return to China right after he finishes his exams in December.

_____

_____

_____

_____

_____

M Write a brief essay on this topic:

What I look for when shopping for clothes: preferences and criteria. PRESENTATIONAL

_____

_____

_____

_____

_____

_____

N Write a story in Chinese based on the four images below. Make sure that your story has a beginning, middle, and end, and that the transition from one picture to the next is smooth and logical. PRESENTATIONAL

_____

_____

_____

_____

_____

Lesson 5

第五课

第五課

选课
選課

Choosing Classes

CHIN 20100
经济 ECON
电脑 CMSC

Check off the following language functions as you learn how to:

[ ] Describe your course workload

[ ] Talk about plans after graduation

[ ] Discuss what will enhance your future job opportunities

[ ] List ways to save money for school

As you progress through the lesson, note other language functions you would like to learn.

_____

_____

_____

Audio

A Listen to the Lesson Text audio, then circle the most appropriate choice. INTERPRETIVE

1 What courses is Zhang Tianming taking this semester?

a world history, math, Chinese, and political science

b computer science, world history, Chinese, and political science

c Chinese, political science, philosophy, and world history

2 What does Zhang Tianming's mother want him to major in?

a medicine

b Chinese

c finance

3 What does Li Zhe plan to do after he graduates from college?

a attend graduate school

b study abroad

c find a job

4 What does Zhang Tianming's mom think he should do in order to become more competitive on the job market?

a do social work

b intern

c study finance

B Listen to the Workbook Dialogue audio, then mark these statements true or false. INTERPRETIVE

1 _____ The speakers are likely a mother and son.

2 _____ The man is not likely to follow his father's post-graduation advice.

3 _____ None of the courses the man is taking next semester will fulfill his major requirements.

4 _____ The man is quite confident about his academic work next semester.

C Based on the Workbook Dialogue audio, circle the most appropriate choice. INTERPRETIVE

1 The woman suggests that the man take another course in computer science because

a it is required for his major.

b it would be easier than a course in finance.

c it is more relevant to his future studies as a graduate student.

2 Taking a philosophy course is required of

a all students.

b all engineering students.

c all graduating seniors.

D Listen to the Workbook Narrative 1 audio, then circle the most appropriate choice. INTERPRETIVE

1 **What schools does the university have?**

    a   Schools of Medicine, Liberal Arts, Engineering, and Architecture

    b   Schools of Management, Engineering, Medicine, and Liberal Arts

    c   Schools of Law, Medicine, Engineering, and Liberal Arts

2 **Which school has the most expensive tuition?**

    a   the School of Medicine

    b   the School of Engineering

    c   the School of Management

3 **Which school has the most students?**

    a   the School of Engineering

    b   the School of Liberal Arts

    c   the School of Medicine

4 **Which school has the largest library?**

    a   the School of Medicine

    b   the School of Management

    c   the School of Liberal Arts

5 **Which school has the best faculty?**

    a   the School of Management

    b   the School of Engineering

    c   the School of Liberal Arts

6 **What is the controversy about?**

    a   tuition

    b   the number of students

    c   the foreign language requirement

E Listen to the Workbook Narrative 2 audio, then mark these statements true or false. INTERPRETIVE

1 ____ The job market has become more competitive because more and more students are graduating from college with double majors.

2 ____ The writer believes that double majoring can be a rewarding experience.

F Listen to the Workbook Narrative 3 audio, then mark these statements true or false. INTERPRETIVE

1 ____ Little Lin's original plan for next semester was to take three courses for twelve credits.

2 ____ Little Lin's parents wanted him to take more courses and double major.

3 ____ Little Lin's professor suggested he take four courses over the summer.

4 ____ Little Lin will follow his professor's advice.

____ Listen to the Workbook Listening Rejoinder audio. After hearing the first speaker, select the best response from the four choices given by the second speaker. Indicate the letter of your choice. INTERPRETIVE

II. Pinyin and Tone

A Compare the pronunciations of the underlined characters in the two words or phrases given. Provide their initials in *pinyin*.

经济/經濟 _____   电脑系/電腦系 _____

B Compare the tones of the underlined characters in the two words or phrases given. Indicate the tones with 1 (first tone), 2 (second tone), 3 (third tone), 4 (fourth tone), or 0 (neutral tone).

教生词/教生詞 _____   教授 _____

III. Speaking

A Practice asking and answering these questions. INTERPERSONAL

1 你这学期选了几门课？
  你這學期選了幾門課？

2 你最喜欢哪一门课？为什么？
  你最喜歡哪一門課？為什麼？

3 哪门课最让你受不了？为什么？
  哪門課最讓你受不了？為什麼？

4 你下个学期打算学几个学分？什么时候可以毕业？
  你下個學期打算學幾個學分？什麼時候可以畢業？

Practice speaking with these prompts. **PRESENTATIONAL**

1 请谈谈你这个学期的学习。

  請談談你這個學期的學習。

2 请谈谈你找谁讨论选专业的事儿。为什么？

  請談談你找誰討論選專業的事兒。為什麼？

3 请谈谈你的专业以及毕业以后的打算。

  請談談你的專業以及畢業以後的打算。

IV. Reading Comprehension

A Complete this section by writing the characters, *pinyin*, and English equivalent of each new word formed. Guess the meaning, then use a dictionary to confirm.

1 "中国"的"国"+"世界"的"界"

  "中國"的"國"+"世界"的"界"

  → 国／國 + 界→ _____ _____ _____

2 "申请"的"申"+"告诉"的"诉"

  "申請"的"申"+"告訴"的"訴"

  → 申 + 诉／訴→ _____ _____ _____

3 "轻松"的"轻"+"方便"的"便"

  "輕鬆"的"輕"+"方便"的"便"

  → 轻／輕 + 便→ _____ _____ _____

4 "数字"的"数"+"化学"的"学"

"數字"的"數"+"化學"的"學"

→ 数/數 ＋ 学/學→ _____ _____ _____

5 "决定"的"决"+"比赛"的"赛"

"決定"的"決"+"比賽"的"賽"

→ 决/決 ＋ 赛/賽→ _____ _____ _____

B Read the passage, then mark the statements true or false. INTERPRETIVE

小李是大学三年级的学生，因为他打算明年五月就毕业，所以每个学期都选六门课，每年暑假都实习。要是学分够，他还打算拿双学位。他的教授觉得他课选得太多了，建议他少选一点，要不然太累了，对身体健康没有好处。小李说他希望早一点毕业，这样他可以把大四一年的钱省下来。累不累，他不在乎。

小李是大學三年級的學生，因為他打算明年五月就畢業，所以每個學期都選六門課，每年暑假都實習。要是學分夠，他還打算拿雙學位。他的教授覺得他課選得太多了，建議他少選一點，要不然太累了，對身體健康沒有好處。小李說他希望早一點畢業，這樣他可以把大四一年的錢省下來。累不累，他不在乎。

1 ＿＿＿ Little Li wants to graduate a year early to save on tuition.

2 ＿＿＿ Little Li has spent every summer taking classes.

3 ＿＿＿ Little Li's professor considers early graduation very important for his future.

4 ＿＿＿ Little Li prioritizes his health over everything.

C Read the passage, then mark the statements true or false. INTERPRETIVE

有一天，几个朋友讨论选专业的事。小王说他的父母一直想让他毕业以后念医学院。小林说她对上工学院很有兴趣，可是她父母觉得还是学医最好。小白说他爸爸妈妈不管他，他学什么专业都可以。小白开始想选历史专业，可是为了跟女朋友小林在一起，也考虑上医学院。小张听了以后就说："你们大家都学医，那我只好学'生病专业'了。要不然，将来你们这么多医生到哪儿去找病人啊？"

有一天，幾個朋友討論選專業的事。小王說他的父母一直想讓他畢業以後念醫學院。小林說她對上工學院很有興趣，可是她父母覺得還是學醫最好。小白說他爸爸媽媽不管他，他學什麼專業都可以。小白開始想選歷史專業，可是為了跟女朋友小林在一起，也考慮上醫學院。小張聽了以後就說："你們大家都學醫，那我只好學'生病專業'了。要不然，將來你們這麼多醫生到哪兒去找病人啊？"

1 ___ 小王的父母不在乎他选什么专业。
　　___ 小王的父母不在乎他選什麼專業。

2 ___ 小林觉得学工比学医有意思。
　　___ 小林覺得學工比學醫有意思。

3 ___ 小林的父母觉得她上医学院比较合适。
　　___ 小林的父母覺得她上醫學院比較合適。

4 ___ 小白的父母希望他学历史。
　　___ 小白的父母希望他學歷史。

5 ___ 小张身体不好，常常生病。
　　___ 小張身體不好，常常生病。

6 ___ 小张觉得学医的人太多了。
　　___ 小張覺得學醫的人太多了。

D Look at the photo, then answer the question in English. **INTERPRETIVE**

What college/school is this? _____

Look at this degree certificate issued by a university in Mainland China, then answer the questions in English. INTERPRETIVE

学生　李大成　系　　　　授予　文　学学士学位

江苏武进人，一九八二年

十一月生。在上海外国语学院

校（院）　　英语　系　　校（院）长　学位评定委员会主席

英语　专业

修业四年，成绩及格，准予

毕业。经审核符合《中华人

民共和国学位条例》规定，

证书编号：

學生　李大成　係　　　　授予　文　學學士學位。

江蘇武進　人，一九八二年

十一月生。在上海外國語學院

校（院）　　英語　系

英語　專業　　校（院）長　　學位評定委員會主席

修業四年，成績及格，准予

畢業。經審核符合《中華人

民共和國學位條例》規定。

證書編號：

1　What is the degree recipient's name? _____

2　What is his date of birth? _____

3　What is the name of the university? _____

4　What is the degree recipient's major? _____

5　How long is the degree program? _____

6　What degree was awarded? _____

7　What role does  serve at the university? _____

8　When was the degree awarded? _____

世界一流大学·医学院

北京·复旦·清华·交通（原上海第二医大）·
首都·政法大学....

申请资格：高中职或专科毕业·大学在学生·学士后医及硕博士研究生

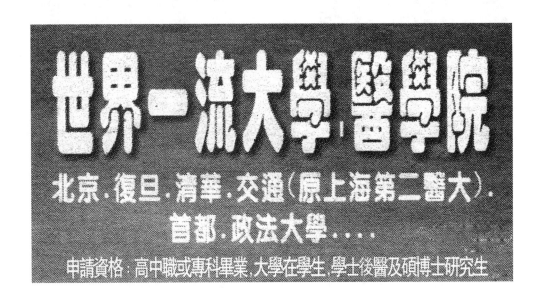

世界一流大學·醫學院

北京·復旦·清華·交通（原上海第二醫大）·
首都·政法大學....

申請資格：高中職或專科畢業·大學在學生·學士後醫及碩博士研究生

这是一个报纸广告。你能申请这些学校吗？你想申请吗？
为什么？

這是一個報紙廣告。你能申請這些學校嗎？你想申請嗎？
為什麼？

_____

_____

_____

_____

_____

A Form a character by combining the given components as instructed. Then use that character to write a word, phrase, or short sentence.

1 上边一个"田"，下边一个"介绍"的"介"，

上邊一個"田"，下邊一個"介紹"的"介"，

是 ＿＿＿＿＿＿ 的 ＿＿＿＿ 。

2 左边一个提手旁，右边一个"受不了"的"受"，

左邊一個提手旁，右邊一個"受不了"的"受"，

是 ＿＿＿＿＿＿ 的 ＿＿＿＿ 。

3 左边一个言字旁，右边一个"寸"，

左邊一個言字旁，右邊一個"寸"，

是 ＿＿＿＿＿＿ 的 ＿＿＿＿ 。

4 上边一个"打折"的"折"，下边一个"口"，

上邊一個"打折"的"折"，下邊一個"口"，

是 ＿＿＿＿＿＿ 的 ＿＿＿＿ 。

B As the saying goes, you can't have it all. What prevents the following scenarios from being perfect? Complete the sentences using 就是 or 只是, following the example below. **PRESENTATIONAL**

这条运动裤质量好，价钱便宜，❌ (style)

這條運動褲質量好，價錢便宜，

→ 这条运动裤质量好，价钱便宜，就是样子不太好看。

→ 這條運動褲質量好，價錢便宜，就是樣子不太好看。

1 中国历史课很有意思，老师也很好，❌ (amount of homework)

中國歷史課很有意思，老師也很好，

2 夏天去上海学中文，时间没问题，那里我也有很多朋友，❌ (affordability)

夏天去上海學中文，時間沒問題，那裡我也有很多朋友，

_____

3 当医生很好，能帮助很多人，挣很多钱，❌ (relaxing)

當醫生很好，能幫助很多人，掙很多錢，

_____

C Based on your own situation and the Textbook Dialogues, fill in the blanks with the correct resultative complements and answer the questions, following the example below. **INTERPERSONAL**

Q: 昨天的功课你做<u>完</u>了吗？
昨天的功課你做<u>完</u>了嗎？

A: <u>昨天的功课我做完了。</u>
<u>昨天的功課我做完了。</u>

or

A: <u>昨天的功课我没做完。</u>
<u>昨天的功課我沒做完。</u>

1 Q: 今天老师上课说的话你听 _____ 了吗？
今天老師上課說的話你聽 _____ 了嗎？

A: _____

2 Q: 张天明买 _____ 他要的运动服了吗？
張天明買 _____ 他要的運動服了嗎？

A: _____

3 Q: 李哲下学期的课选 _____ 了吗？
李哲下學期的課選 _____ 了嗎？

A: _____

D Complete the dialogues using 另外 (the other), following the example below. **INTERPERSONAL**

Q: 你的同屋都是新生吗？
你的同屋都是新生嗎？

A: 我有三个同屋，两个新生，<u>另外一个是老生</u>。
我有三個同屋，兩個新生，<u>另外一個是老生</u>。

1 Q: 这附近有几家购物中心？离这儿远吗？
這附近有幾家購物中心？離這兒遠嗎？

A: 有两家。一家很近，_____。
有兩家。一家很近，_____。

2 Q: 我们放三天假，你打算做什么？
我們放三天假，你打算做什麼？

A: 我打算一天洗衣服，_____。
我打算一天洗衣服，_____。

3 Q: 他的三个弟弟都大学毕业了吧？
他的三個弟弟都大學畢業了吧？

A: 他的大弟已经毕业了，_____。
他的大弟已經畢業了，_____。

Complete the dialogues using 另外 (besides), following the example below. INTERPERSONAL

Q: 这层楼有什么?
   這層樓有什麼？

A: 这层楼有洗衣机和干衣机，另外还有电脑。
   這層樓有洗衣機和乾衣機，另外還有電腦。

1 Q: 你这学期上什么课?
     你這學期上什麼課？

  A: 我这学期上中文，＿＿＿＿＿＿＿＿＿＿＿。
     我這學期上中文，＿＿＿＿＿＿＿＿＿＿。

2 Q: 张天明、丽莎、柯林和林雪梅四个人去中国饭馆儿吃
     饭，点了些什么菜?
     張天明、麗莎、柯林和林雪梅四個人去中國飯館兒吃
     飯，點了些什麼菜？

  A: 他们点了芥兰牛肉，＿＿＿＿＿＿＿＿＿＿。
     他們點了芥蘭牛肉，＿＿＿＿＿＿＿＿＿。

3 Q: 林雪梅和丽莎需要买些什么日用品?
     林雪梅和麗莎需要買些什麼日用品？

  A: 她们需要买卫生纸、牙膏，＿＿＿＿＿＿＿＿＿＿。
     她們需要買衛生紙、牙膏，＿＿＿＿＿＿＿＿＿。

F Use the images and 要么…，要么…/要麼…，要麼… to complete the dialogues.
INTERPERSONAL

1  Q: 这个周末你打算做什么?
                       這個週末你打算做什麼？

                    A: ＿＿＿＿＿＿＿＿＿＿＿＿＿＿＿＿＿

2
Q: 你今天晚饭想吃什么？
你今天晚飯想吃什麼？

A: _____

3
Q: 你希望妈妈送给你什么生日礼物？
你希望媽媽送給你什麼生日禮物？

A: _____

G Complete the dialogues using the terms in parentheses and 跟…打交道, following the example below. INTERPERSONAL

Q: 你为什么不念医学院？ (patients)
你為什麼不念醫學院？

A: 因为我不愿意跟病人打交道。
因為我不願意跟病人打交道。

1 Q: 你为什么不当售货员了？ (money, customers)
你為什麼不當售貨員了？

A: _____

2 Q: 你的专业是金融，这份工作对你很合适，怎么不申请？ (numbers)
你的專業是金融，這份工作對你很合適，怎麼不申請？

A: _____

3 Q: 快开学了，学校需要一些老生帮新生搬进宿舍，你的
同屋为什么不愿意帮忙？ (freshmen)
快開學了，學校需要一些老生幫新生搬進宿舍，你的
同屋為什麼不願意幫忙？

A: _____

H Translate these sentences into Chinese. **PRESENTATIONAL**

1 **Person A:** Have you finished choosing classes for next semester?

_____

Person B: Yes, I've finished. I've chosen Chinese, chemistry, economics, and world history. How about you? Have you finished choosing?

_____

_____

Person A: I also want to take Chinese and chemistry. I haven't thought through the other two courses. I'll see my professor tomorrow. I'd like to hear her opinion.

_____

_____

2 **Person A:** This tracksuit is really nice.

_____

Person B: It is very nice. It's just that the price is too high.

_____

Person A: I'd also like to save money. But the quality of the other tracksuits is too poor.

_____

Person B: Will you buy it no matter how expensive it is?

_____

Person A: Either you buy things of good quality or you don't buy anything at all. I don't care about price.

_____

I Translate these passages into Chinese. PRESENTATIONAL

1 My major is computer science. I am graduating next year. But I haven't done any internships before, so I've decided to work part-time at a computer company this winter break.

_____

_____

2 Little Lin spent a lot of time preparing for exams and writing papers this week. He felt it was too much to bear. He hopes he won't have to worry about studying this weekend and he can have fun.

_____

_____

3 My older brother plans to go to graduate or medical school after he graduates next semester. He says he will study either engineering or medicine. My parents hope that my older brother will study computer science and make a lot of money in the future. They know that he can make even more money if he goes to medical school. However, they don't want my older brother to deal with patients all day long. My older brother says he doesn't care if he makes a lot of money or not. He just wants to do what he loves/likes.

_____

_____

_____

_____

J Write a report on your studies in Chinese. Include information on the courses you have taken and are taking, the number of credits you need to graduate, your major (or prospective major) and the reason you're interested in it, whether your parents have influenced your choice of major, your outlook on graduate work or job prospects after graduating from college, and any other relevant information. PRESENTATIONAL

_____

_____

_____

_____

K Write a story in Chinese based on the four images below. Make sure that your story has a beginning, middle, and end, and that the transition from one picture to the next is smooth and logical. **PRESENTATIONAL**

_____

_____

_____

_____

_____

Bringing It Together (Lessons 1–5)

A Write down the correct pronunciation, including tones, of the following short sentences in *pinyin*. Use a computer or smartphone to record yourself speaking. If you've been asked to do so, send the recording to your teacher. Then translate each sentence into English. **INTERPRETIVE**

1 学校离家很远。
  學校離家很遠。

  _____

  _____

2 学生公寓很安全。
  學生公寓很安全。

  _____

  _____

3 住在校外的好处不少。
  住在校外的好處不少。

  _____

  _____

4 这栋楼比较旧。
  這棟樓比較舊。

  _____

  _____

5 靠窗户摆着一台洗衣机。
　　靠窗戶擺著一台洗衣機。

_____

_____

6 过马路别着急。
　　過馬路別著急。

_____

_____

7 那个留学生是研究生。
　　那個留學生是研究生。

_____

_____

8 这盘红烧鸡又油又咸。
　　這盤紅燒雞又油又鹹。

_____

_____

9 这条牛仔裤的质量挺好。
　　這條牛仔褲的質量挺好。

_____

_____

10 你的购物标准是什么？

你的購物標準是什麼？

_____

_____

11 她非买名牌的衣服不可。

她非買名牌的衣服不可。

_____

_____

12 在这里无论买什么都得付税。

在這裡無論買什麼都得付稅。

_____

_____

13 小高考虑选金融做专业。

小高考慮選金融做專業。

_____

_____

14 教授建议这件事明天再讨论。

教授建議這件事明天再討論。

_____

_____

II. Applying Your Chinese

A While studying abroad in China, you run into the following scenarios. **PRESENTATIONAL**

1 You're at a grocery store. What food items and cooking ingredients can you name?

_____

_____

_____

2 You're at a Chinese restaurant. What dishes can you name without looking them up?

Meat dishes: _____

Vegetarian dishes: _____

Soups: _____

Spicy dishes: _____

Beverages: _____

3 You're in a convenience store getting some daily necessities. What items can you name without asking your Chinese friends?

_____

_____

_____

4 You're in a clothing store. What pieces of clothing can you ask the salesperson to show you?

_____

_____

_____

5 You're flipping through the academic directory of a Chinese university. What departments/schools can you identify?

_____

_____

_____

Engage in some personal brainstorming and fill out the provided lists in Chinese. After you've finished, compare notes with one of your classmates. **PRESENTATIONAL & INTERPERSONAL**

1 Information that you want people to know about you when you first meet:

_____

_____

_____

_____

2 Your opinions about on-campus and off-campus living:

On-campus living

Pros: _____

_____

Cons: _____

_____

Off-campus living

Pros: _____

_____

Cons: _____

_____

3 Your dietary restrictions and/or preferences:

Restrictions: _____

_____

Preferences: _____

_____

4   Your preferences and criteria when shopping for clothes, with the most important listed first:

_____   _____   _____   _____   _____

most important   least important

5   Academic courses and additional career-planning resources that you think might help your future job prospects:

_____

_____

_____

_____

After you have finished filling out your lists, interview a classmate about his/her opinions on these topics.

C   Based on, but not limited to, the information you provided in (A) and (B) of this section, present an oral report or write a paragraph in Chinese in response to each of the following questions.

PRESENTATIONAL

1   What advice would you give if asked whether it would be better to live on campus or off campus?

2   How would you describe the interior and surroundings of your ideal living quarters?

3   Suppose your personal chef is to prepare a Chinese meal for you. What instructions would you give him/her?

4   Suppose your personal assistant is going to shop for a new outfit for you. What instructions would you give him/her?

5   Suppose you're a career counselor. What advice would you give students to help them be more competitive on the job market after graduation?

男朋友女朋友

Dating

 Check off the following language functions as you learn how to:

[ ] Compare your interests with your friends

[ ] Show concern, ask if things are OK, and investigate further if necessary

[ ] Give a simple description of the traits you look for in friends

[ ] Tell what makes you anxious or angry

As you progress through the lesson, note other language functions you would like to learn.

_____

_____

_____

A Listen to the Lesson Text audio, then circle the most appropriate choice. INTERPRETIVE

1 **Zhang Tianming and Lisha first met**

    a in high school.

    b on their first day at college.

    c at a Chinese restaurant.

2 **What does Xuemei want to find out by visiting Lisha this evening?**

    a Lisha's cultural background

    b whether Zhang Tianming has a new girlfriend

    c what Lisha and Zhang Tianming fought over

3 **What did Zhang Tianming do that made Lisha so unhappy?**

    a He refused to take Lisha to a concert.

    b He went to a movie by himself without waiting for Lisha.

    c He seemed to be forgetful about their dates.

4 **What do we know about Xuemei's relationship with Ke Lin?**

    a She has never mentioned their relationship to her parents.

    b They have never argued with each other.

    c Ke Lin has never helped celebrate her birthday.

5 **Why does Xuemei mention Ke Lin's absent-mindedness to Lisha?**

    a to complain about her boyfriend

    b to make Lisha feel she is not alone

    c to explain why she has not told her parents about her boyfriend

B Listen to the Workbook Dialogue audio, then mark these statements true or false. INTERPRETIVE

1 ____ **The two speakers are in front of a movie theater.**

2 ____ **Tianming calls after waiting for twenty minutes.**

3 ____ **Lisha is about to call Tianming when he calls her.**

4 ____ **Lisha lost track of time because she was watching a concert on TV.**

5 ____ **Lisha arrives at the movie theater around 7:55.**

6 ____ **Lisha couldn't find Tianming because there were too many people there.**

7 ____ **In the end, Tianming realizes that he is not in a position to forgive Lisha.**

C Listen to the Workbook Narrative 1 audio, then mark these statements true or false. INTERPRETIVE

1 _____ Little Wang was very unhappy yesterday because he couldn't find anyone to play ball with him.

2 _____ Little Wang's friends invited him to play ball in order to cheer him up.

3 _____ Little Wang thinks about his girlfriend the whole time while playing ball.

4 _____ Little Wang's girlfriend is angry, but Little Wang seems happy.

D Listen to the Workbook Narrative 2 audio, then circle the most appropriate choice. INTERPRETIVE

1 In what ways does Little Li differ from her good friend?

  a Their cultural backgrounds are similar, but their hobbies are different.

  b Their hobbies are similar, but their cultural backgrounds are different.

  c Both their hobbies and cultural backgrounds are different.

2 What are their respective hobbies?

  a Little Li loves shopping and her friend is a sports buff.

  b Little Li loves music and her friend is a sports buff.

  c Little Li loves music and her friend is a movie buff.

3 Which of the following describes their relationship most accurately?

  a They do everything together despite having different hobbies.

  b They try to change each other's hobbies.

  c They allow each other to do things on their own.

E Listen to the Workbook Narrative 3 audio, then mark these statements true or false. INTERPRETIVE

1 _____ Xiaoming is a sophomore in college but doesn't yet know how to drive.

2 _____ Xiaoming is concerned about his forgetfulness.

3 _____ Xiaoming's mother is worried about his chances of finding a girlfriend.

F _____ Listen to the Workbook Listening Rejoinder audio. After hearing the first speaker, select the best response from the four choices given by the second speaker. Indicate the letter of your choice. INTERPRETIVE

A   Compare the pronunciations of the underlined characters in the two words or phrases given. Provide their initials in *pinyin*.

实<u>际</u>上/實<u>際</u>上 _____   生<u>气</u>/生<u>氣</u> _____

B   Compare the tones of the underlined characters in the two words or phrases given. Indicate the tones with 1 (first tone), 2 (second tone), 3 (third tone), 4 (fourth tone), or 0 (neutral tone).

好<u>处</u>/好<u>處</u> _____   爱<u>好</u>/愛<u>好</u> _____

III. Speaking

A   Practice asking and answering these questions. **INTERPERSONAL**

1   什么事会让你着急?
    什麼事會讓你著急？

2   什么事会让你生气?
    什麼事會讓你生氣？

3   你对什么有兴趣?
    你對什麼有興趣？

4   你觉得班上同学谁比较开朗?
    你覺得班上同學誰比較開朗？

5   你家里谁常常忘这忘那，丢三拉四?
    你家裡誰常常忘這忘那，丟三拉四？

Practice speaking with these prompts. **PRESENTATIONAL**

1 请谈一谈自己的兴趣和爱好。

请谈一谈自己的興趣和愛好。

2 请谈一谈你交朋友的标准。

請談一談你交朋友的標準。

3 In pairs, perform a role-play. Your friend is trying to persuade you to go on a blind date with someone and attempts to present the person in the best possible light by telling you about his/her hobbies and interests, special skills, personality, etc. You, however, are wary. You have a lot of questions about the person that you'd like your friend to answer.

IV. Reading Comprehension

A Complete this section by writing the characters, *pinyin*, and English equivalent of each new word formed. Guess the meaning, then use a dictionary to confirm.

1 "下雪"的"雪"+"篮球"的"球"

"下雪"的"雪"+"籃球"的"球"

→ 雪 + 球→ _____ _____ _____

2 "背景"的"背"+"电影院"的"影"

"背景"的"背"+"電影院"的"影"

→ 背 + 影→ _____ _____ _____

3 "打球"的"打"+"吵架"的"架"

→ 打 + 架→ _____ _____ _____

4 "道歉"的"歉"+"意思"的"意"

→ 歉 + 意→ _____ _____ _____

5 "丢三拉四"的"丢"+"脸圆圆的"的"脸"

"丢三拉四"的"丢"+"臉圓圓的"的"臉"

→ 丢 + 脸/臉→ _____ _____ _____

Fill in the blanks with the phrases provided. **INTERPRETIVE**

想来想去/想來想去   走来走去/走來走去

找来找去/找來找去   考虑来考虑去/考慮來考慮去

等来等去/等來等去

1 小梅病了，她的男朋友来看她，可是醫生正在给她
检查，不能进去。他在外边着急地 _____，
不知道什么时候可以进去。

小梅病了，她的男朋友來看她，可是醫生正在給她
檢查，不能進去。他在外邊著急地 _____，
不知道什麼時候可以進去。

2 老王常常忘这忘那，东西乱放，昨天钥匙不见了，
_____，原来在冰箱里。

老王常常忘這忘那，東西亂放，昨天鑰匙不見了，
_____，原來在冰箱裡。

3 大家约好了一起坐地铁去看演唱会，可是 _____
_____，小林还不来，大家都很生气。

大家約好了一起坐地鐵去看演唱會，可是 _____
_____，小林還不來，大家都很生氣。

4 这个问题很大，公司里的人 _____ 还是没办法
解决。

這個問題很大，公司裡的人 _____ 還是沒辦法
解决。

5 表哥快大学毕业了，_____，最后决定找工作，
不念研究生了。

表哥快大學畢業了，_____，最後決定找工作，
不念研究生了。

Read the passage, then mark the statements true or false. INTERPRETIVE

张天明的父母都很开朗，两个人一直相处得很好。他们都很爱交朋友，兴趣也差不多一样，比方说他们都喜欢听音乐、跳舞。他们也都爱旅行，去过世界很多地方。另外，两个人都喜欢看电视。不过张先生是个篮球迷，喜欢看篮球赛。张太太对篮球一点儿兴趣都没有，但特别喜欢看滑冰比赛。晚上的电视如果又有篮球比赛又有滑冰比赛的话，张太太就只好让张先生看，自己给朋友打电话聊天儿。可是有的时候张先生为了让太太高兴，也只好不看篮球赛，陪太太一起看滑冰。所以他们两个人很少吵架。

张天明昨天晚上看电视的时候想到爸爸妈妈看电视的事儿，就给爸爸打电话，让爸爸给妈妈再买一个电视，送给妈妈当生日礼物。

张天明的父母都很開朗，兩個人一直相處得很好。他們都很愛交朋友，興趣也差不多一樣，比方說他們都喜歡聽音樂、跳舞。他們也都愛旅行，去過世界很多地方。另外，兩個人都喜歡看電視。不過張先生是個籃球迷，喜歡看籃球賽。張太太對籃球一點兒興趣都沒有，但特別喜歡看滑冰比賽。晚上的電視如果又有籃球比賽又有滑冰比賽的話，張太太就只好讓張先生看，自己給朋友打電話聊天兒。可是有的時候張先生為了讓太太高興，也只好不看籃球賽，陪太太一起看滑冰。所以他們兩個人很少吵架。

張天明昨天晚上看電視的時候想到爸爸媽媽看電視的事兒，就給爸爸打電話，讓爸爸給媽媽再買一個電視，送給媽媽當生日禮物。

1 ____ Mr. and Mrs. Zhang are more similar than different in terms of personality and interests.

2 ____ Mr. and Mrs. Zhang like to watch different TV programs.

3 ____ They like to travel, listen to music, dance, watch TV, and hang out with friends.

4 ____ Mr. Zhang makes Mrs. Zhang call her friends whenever there's a basketball game on TV.

5 ____ Mr. Zhang sometimes watches ice skating to make his wife happy.

6 ____ The secret to their successful marriage is having two TVs.

Read the passage, then complete the task. **INTERPRETIVE**

　　小白的父亲一直希望小白在大学好好儿学习，不要交男朋友。可是小白上个星期打电话回家，告诉父亲她交男朋友了，他叫汤姆。小白说，虽然汤姆的文化背景跟她不一样，可是很开朗，长得也挺帅。白先生听了决定自己去看看。昨天是星期六，白先生开车来到小白上学的城市，约好十二点半在一家中国餐馆儿跟汤姆见面，可是汤姆一点钟才到。小白很着急，一问，才知道他跑到一家日本餐馆儿去了。白先生很生气。他觉得汤姆这样马虎，跟小白不会相处得很好。可是汤姆不停地道歉，白先生觉得汤姆态度特别好，所以就同意他们两个人交朋友了。

　　小白的父親一直希望小白在大學好好兒學習，不要交男朋友。可是小白上個星期打電話回家，告訴父親她交男朋友了，他叫湯姆。小白說，雖然湯姆的文化背景跟她不一樣，可是很開朗，長得也挺帥。白先生聽了決定自己去看看。昨天是星期六，白先生開車來到小白上學的城市，約好十二點半在一家中國餐館兒跟湯姆見面，可是湯姆一點鐘才到。小白很著急，一問，才知道他跑到一家日本餐館兒去了。白先生很生氣。他覺得湯姆這樣馬虎，跟小白不會相處得很好。可是湯姆不停地道歉，白先生覺得湯姆態度特別好，所以就同意他們兩個人交朋友了。

In English, list Tom's positive attributes in the ✅ column and his negative attributes in the ❌ column.

✅	❌
_____	_____
_____	_____
_____	_____
_____	_____

Fill in the blanks with 的, 得, or 地. **INTERPRETIVE**

小王上个星期跟教授约好昨天上午九点讨论选课＿＿＿事。可是他把这件事忘＿＿＿一干二净。今天中午在餐厅碰见教授，小王才想起来，他就不停＿＿＿给教授道歉。教授生气＿＿＿看了看小王，一句话也没说，很快＿＿＿走出了餐厅。

小王上個星期跟教授約好昨天上午九點討論選課＿＿＿事。可是他把這件事忘＿＿＿一乾二淨。今天中午在餐廳碰見教授，小王才想起來，他就不停＿＿＿給教授道歉。教授生氣＿＿＿看了看小王，一句話也沒說，很快＿＿＿走出了餐廳。

F Answer the questions in English based on this movie theater advertisement. **INTERPRETIVE**

近期活动
1、周一咖啡日；周二电影全天半价；周一周三爆米花特价卖；周四观影女士半价；周五、六夜场通宵连放；
2、持本人老年证、本人学生证（23周岁以下）观影半价；
3、每天中午12:30前22:00后观影半价。

近期活動
1、週一咖啡日；週二電影全天半價；週一週三爆米花特價賣；週四觀影女士半價；週五、六夜場通宵連放；
2、持本人老年證、本人學生證（23週歲以下）觀影半價；
3、每天中午12:30前22:00後觀影半價。

1 On which day of the week would you want to catch a movie? Why?

_____

2 What discount does the movie theater offer to senior citizens?

_____

3 What discount does it offer for morning shows?

_____

姓名	王小梅	星座	双子座
性别	♀	出生年月	1990 年 6 月 14 日
身高	165 cm	体重	48 kg
所在城市	北京	老家	海淀
国籍	中国	血型	O 型
婚姻状况	未婚	体型	保密
休息日	双休六日	月收入	保密
学历	大学专科	毕业学校	北京医科大学
兄妹情况	兄妹两人以上	专业	眼科
工作情况	在职	从事职业	医生
吸烟	不吸		
喝酒	偶尔		
住房	与父母同住	汽车	有买车计划
擅长（爱好）	听音乐、跑步		
性格自介	活泼开朗,外向,温柔体贴,不拘小节,害羞,老实,敏感,快言快语		

姓名	王小梅	星座	雙子座
性別	♀	出生年月	1990 年 6 月 14 日
身高	165 cm	體重	48 kg
所在城市	北京	老家	海淀
國籍	中國	血型	O 型
婚姻狀況	未婚	體型	保密
休息日	雙休六日	月收入	保密
學歷	大學專科	畢業學校	北京醫科大學
兄妹情況	兄妹兩人以上	專業	眼科
工作情況	在職	從事職業	醫生
吸煙	不吸		
喝酒	偶爾		
住房	與父母同住	汽車	有買車計劃
擅長(愛好)	聽音樂、跑步		
性格自介	活潑開朗,外向,溫柔體貼,不拘小節,害羞,老實,敏感,快言快語		

1 ___ She lives in Beijing with her parents.

2 ___ She doesn't have any siblings.

3 ___ She's never been married.

4 ___ She graduated from medical school.

5 ___ She gets one day off from work every week.

6 ___ She owns a car.

7 ___ She considers herself outgoing.

V. Writing and Grammar

A Form a character by combining the given components as indicated. Then use that character to write a word, phrase, or short sentence.

1 上边一个"加"，下边一个"木"，

上邊一個"加"，下邊一個"木"，

是 ＿＿＿＿＿＿＿ 的 ＿＿＿＿ 。

2 左边一个"木"，右边一个"目"，

左邊一個"木"，右邊一個"目"，

是 ＿＿＿＿＿＿＿ 的 ＿＿＿＿ 。

3 上边一个"北"，下边一个"月"，

上邊一個"北"，下邊一個"月"，

是 ＿＿＿＿＿＿＿ 的 ＿＿＿＿ 。

4 上边一个"日"，下边一个"北京"的"京"，

上邊一個"日"，下邊一個"北京"的"京"，

是 ＿＿＿＿＿＿＿ 的 ＿＿＿＿ 。

B Clear up the confusion surrounding the IC characters by first asking questions using 到底, then answering based on the text. Follow the example below. **PRESENTATIONAL**

(on campus   VS.   off campus)

Q: 张天明到底住校内还是住校外？
张天明到底住校內還是住校外？

A: 他住校内。
他住校內。

1

(undergraduate student   VS.   graduate student)

Q: _____

A: _____

2

(spicy food   VS.   sweet food)

Q: _____

A: _____

3

(hot-and-sour soup   VS.   spinach-and-tofu soup)

Q: _____

A: _____

4  (tracksuit　　　　　VS.　　　jeans)

Q: _____

A: _____

5 (find a job　　　　　VS.　　　go to graduate school)

Q: _____

A: _____

C Paraphrase these sentences using 原来/原來 (originally), following the example below.

PRESENTATIONAL

三年前我认识他的时候，他在学日文，过了几个月就不学了。

三年前我認識他的時候，他在學日文，過了幾個月就不學了。

→ 他原来学日文，后来不学了。

→ 他原來學日文，後來不學了。

1　他上高中的时候，常常运动，上大学以后，就不运动了。

　他上高中的時候，常常運動，上大學以後，就不運動了。

2 他小时候常常吃肉，现在只吃素菜，不吃肉了。

他小時候常常吃肉，現在只吃素菜，不吃肉了。

_____

3 小柯想点清蒸鱼，但是卖完了，只好叫了三十个饺子。

小柯想點清蒸魚，但是賣完了，只好叫了三十個餃子。

_____

D What new information about the IC characters surprised you? Use 原来/原來 (as it turns out) to describe your realization, following the example below. **PRESENTATIONAL**

我以为张天明是在大学认识的丽莎，<u>原来他们在高中的时候就认识了</u>。

我以為張天明是在大學認識的麗莎，<u>原來他們在高中的時候就認識了</u>。

1 我以为柯林是大学一年级的新生，_____
_____。

我以為柯林是大學一年級的新生，_____
_____。

2 我以为张天明对金融很有兴趣，_____
_____。

我以為張天明對金融很有興趣，_____
_____。

3 我以为丽莎是个球迷，_____。

我以為麗莎是個球迷，_____。

4 我以为林雪梅已经把她交男朋友的事儿告诉家里了，
_____。

我以為林雪梅已經把她交男朋友的事兒告訴家裡了，
_____。

Translate these sentences into Chinese. **PRESENTATIONAL**

1 I thought he didn't like the sweet-and-sour fish I made. As it turned out, he was allergic to fish.

_____

2 In terms of hobbies, my roommate and I both like singing and dancing. But in terms of academic studies, I like to deal with numbers, but she doesn't.

_____

3 Why not give the taxi company a call? You never know, perhaps they have found your keys.

_____

4 My roommate was especially busy yesterday afternoon. He was cooking one minute, doing laundry the next, and tidying up the room.

_____

_____

F Translate these dialogues into Chinese. **PRESENTATIONAL**

1 **Person A:**   How's your boyfriend?

_____

Person B: Don't bring him up. He doesn't care about me at all.

_____

Person A: What happened? Does he have another girlfriend?

_____

Person B: No. Every day all he wants to do is play basketball with his friends. He's only got basketball on his mind. Last Saturday evening we had a date to see a movie. Who knew? He played basketball with his friends all night long and totally forgot about the movie. How could I not have gotten angry?

_____

_____

Person A: Is that so? Next time, ask him out on a date to watch a basketball game. Show up half an hour late. Keep him waiting.

_____

Person B: That's a good idea.

_____

2 Person A: How is your roommate?

_____

Person B: Very outgoing and very nice to me. He often helps me practice Chinese. He's just a bit careless.

_____

Person A: Careless in what way?

_____

Person B: He often forgets this or that, or leaves things behind. Last month he bought a T-shirt for me as a birthday gift, but he didn't realize until he gave it to me that the T-shirt was for his girlfriend. He had also bought one for her. Two nights ago he invited me and another good friend of his to dinner. When it was time to pay, I saw he was very embarrassed. Turned out he had forgotten to bring his credit card. I ended up paying.

_____

_____

_____

Person A: He is careless.

_____

G Translate these passages into Chinese. **PRESENTATIONAL**

1 Something seemed to be bothering my younger sister. I asked her repeatedly what it was before she said that she had quarreled with her boyfriend Little Zhang. Little Zhang is a nice guy. He's tall and handsome, and very outgoing. What really happened between the two? It turns out that many girls like Little Zhang, and my sister thought Little Zhang liked them, too. She was not sure if Little Zhang genuinely cared about her.

_____

_____

_____

_____

2 My grandma and grandpa used to fight all the time. My grandpa is a basketball fan. Whenever there is a game on TV, he has to watch it. My grandma is a fan of pop music. Whenever there is a concert on TV, she'll insist on watching it, too. But they only had one TV, so my dad bought another TV. Grandma and Grandpa then each watched their own TVs, and didn't fight anymore.

_____

_____

_____

_____

_____

H In Chinese, list the qualities that you do and don't look for in friends. PRESENTATIONAL

✅	❌
_____	_____
_____	_____
_____	_____
_____	_____
_____	_____
_____	_____
_____	_____

I Imagine that you are helping your older brother or sister join an online dating site. Fill out this form.

INTERPRETIVE & PRESENTATIONAL

留学人员征婚需填表格

姓 名		性 别		出生日期		民 族	
籍 贯		身 高		相 貌		学 历	
爱 好		职 业				所在国	
居留身份				婚姻状况			
有无子女				身体状况			
通讯地址						电 话	
其它情况							
要求对方							

留學人員征婚需填表格

姓 名		性 別		出生日期		民 族	
籍 貫		身 高		相 貌		學 歷	
愛 好		職 業				所在國	
居留身份				婚姻狀況			
有無子女				身體狀況			
通訊地址						電 話	
其它情況							
要求對方							

J Imagine you are going to help your brother or sister send in a ninety-second video clip to an online matchmaking agency in China. Before shooting the video, write a draft of what he/she wants to say about himself/herself and what he/she looks for in an ideal girlfriend or boyfriend. Make sure to include basic information such as his/her name, where he/she is from, education, etc., and personal traits that are important to him/her. PRESENTATIONAL

K Write a story in Chinese based on the four images below. Make sure that your story has a beginning, middle, and end, and make sure that the transition from one picture to the next is smooth and logical. PRESENTATIONAL

_____

_____

_____

_____

_____

电脑和网络
電腦和網絡

Computers and the Internet

✔ Check off the following language functions as you learn how to:

[ ] Name the activities you use the Internet for

[ ] Discuss the pros and cons of using the Internet

[ ] Inquire if others are angry with you

[ ] Recount how you've been inconvenienced by others

As you progress through the lesson, note other language functions you would like to learn.

_____

_____

_____

I. Listening Comprehension

A Listen to the Lesson Text audio, then mark these statements true or false. INTERPRETIVE

1 ____ Zhang Tianming is late for the appointment because he didn't receive an email.

2 ____ Xuemei's professor does not completely trust information on the Internet.

3 ____ Lisha tells Tianming to find a girlfriend online.

4 ____ Zhang Tianming prefers email to the phone because email saves both time and money.

5 ____ Lin Xuemei uses the phone much more than email.

B Listen to the Workbook Dialogue audio, then mark these statements true or false. INTERPRETIVE

1 ____ Tianming was online for half an hour before he developed a stomachache.

2 ____ Tianming ordered stomachache medicine online.

3 ____ Lisha does not believe that all information from the Internet is uniformly reliable.

4 ____ In the end, Tianming may have to agree that Lisha's view of online information is not so irrelevant after all.

5 ____ Tianming didn't see a doctor for his stomachache because he couldn't wait for Lisha to take him.

C Listen to the Workbook Narrative 1 audio, then mark these statements true or false. INTERPRETIVE

1 ____ The speaker urges people to get rid of their computers.

2 ____ The speaker believes that computers' usefulness has been exaggerated.

3 ____ According to the speaker, excessive computer use is detrimental to health.

D Listen to the Workbook Narrative 2 audio, then circle the most appropriate choice. INTERPRETIVE

1 The speaker is

a a father addressing his children.

b a boss addressing his subordinates.

c a professor addressing his students.

2 The speaker thinks that information from the Internet is

a completely reliable.

b not as reliable as information from books and journals.

c completely unreliable.

3 What will the speaker do next?

a He will collect writing assignments from everyone.

b He will give a lecture.

c He will take everyone to the library.

E   Listen to the Workbook Narrative 3 audio, then circle the most appropriate choice. INTERPRETIVE

    1 **Who is the speaker?**

        a   Tianming's girlfriend

        b   Tianming's classmate

        c   Tianming's sister

    2 **This message was**

        a   left on a landline answering machine.

        b   left as voicemail on a cell phone.

        c   sent over email.

    3 **Why didn't Tianming answer the speaker's repeated calls?**

        a   His cell phone was off.

        b   His line was busy.

        c   He didn't have his cell phone with him

    4 **How would you describe the speaker's mood?**

        a   happy

        b   angry

        c   sad

F   _____   Listen to the Workbook Listening Rejoinder audio. After hearing the first speaker, select the best response from the four choices given by the second speaker. Indicate the letter of your choice. INTERPRETIVE

II. Pinyin and Tone

A   Compare the pronunciations of the underlined characters in the two words or phrases given. Provide their initials in _pinyin_.

    软<u>件</u>/軟<u>件</u> _____   网<u>站</u>/網<u>站</u> _____

B   Compare the tones of the underlined characters in the two words or phrases given. Indicate the tones with 1 (first tone), 2 (second tone), 3 (third tone), 4 (fourth tone), or 0 (neutral tone).

    垃<u>圾</u> _____   丢三<u>拉</u>四 _____

A Practice asking and answering these questions. INTERPERSONAL

1 你的电脑从早到晚都开着吗？为什么？

你的電腦從早到晚都開著嗎？為什麼？

2 你每天上网上多长时间？

你每天上網上多長時間？

3 你上网做些什么？

你上網做些什麼？

4 你的生活离得开离不开电脑？

你的生活離得開離不開電腦？

5 要是你的朋友玩儿电脑玩儿上瘾了，你会跟他（or 她）说什么？

要是你的朋友玩兒電腦玩兒上瘾了，你會跟他（or 她）說什麼？

B Practice speaking with these prompts. PRESENTATIONAL

1 请谈谈电脑或者网络给你的生活带来了什么好处。

請談談電腦或者網絡給你的生活帶來了什麼好處。

2 请谈谈电脑或者网络给你的生活带来了什么坏处。

請談談電腦或者網絡給你的生活帶來了什麼壞處。

3 Your friend is hooked on Internet games and has stopped caring about eating or sleeping. It's time for an intervention. Remind him/her about the things that truly matter.

IV. Reading Comprehension

A Complete this section by writing the characters, *pinyin,* and English equivalent of each new word formed. Guess the meaning, then use a dictionary to confirm.

1 "网络"的"网"+"电脑迷"的"迷"

   "網絡"的"網"+"電腦迷"的"迷"

   → 网/網 + 迷→_____ _____ _____

2 "约好"的"约"+"开会"的"会"

   "約好"的"約"+"開會"的"會"

   → 约/約 + 会/會→_____ _____ _____

3 "急忙"的"急"+"生病"的"病"

   → 急 + 病→_____ _____ _____

4 "软件"的"软"+"卧室"的"卧"

   "軟件"的"軟"+"臥室"的"臥"

   → 软/軟 + 卧/臥→_____ _____ _____

5 "落伍"的"落"+"后面"的"后"

   "落伍"的"落"+"後面"的"後"

   → 落/落 + 后/後→_____ _____ _____

B Read the dialogue, then mark the statements true or false. INTERPRETIVE

妈妈： 大明，七点了，你三点半就上网，到现在
       已经三个多小时了。

儿子： 七点了？糟糕，我跟小美约好七点一起去
       听演唱会，又要迟到了。

妈妈： 你这孩子！看你急急忙忙的样子。七点要
       去听演唱会，为什么不早点儿准备？

儿子：我上网下载几个软件，一忙起来就忘了时间了。妈，我的汽车钥匙呢？

妈妈：钥匙不是在你手上吗？你老是这么丢三拉四的，真让我着急。每次约会都迟到，害得小美等你，她能不生气吗？

儿子：没关系，我会好好儿给她道歉的。再说，我下载的软件，有一个是给她的。

妈妈：每天都是上网下载软件！我看你不用交女朋友了，从网上下载一个女朋友算了。

媽媽：大明，七點了，你三點半就上網，到現在已經三個多小時了。

兒子：七點了？糟糕，我跟小美約好七點一起去聽演唱會，又要遲到了。

媽媽：你這孩子！看你急急忙忙的樣子。七點要去聽演唱會，為什麼不早點兒準備？

兒子：我上網下載幾個軟件，一忙起來就忘了時間了。媽，我的汽車鑰匙呢？

媽媽：鑰匙不是在你手上嗎？你老是這麼丟三拉四的，真讓我著急。每次約會都遲到，害得小美等你，她能不生氣嗎？

兒子：沒關係，我會好好兒給她道歉的。再說，我下載的軟件，有一個是給她的。

媽媽：每天都是上網下載軟件！我看你不用交女朋友了，從網上下載一個女朋友算了。

1 ____ Daming is going to be late for the concert.

2 ____ Daming's mother urges her son to hurry up.

3 ____ When Daming uses the Internet, he forgets about everything else.

4   ___   Daming looks for his car key, but he's actually been holding it in his hand.

5   ___   According to Daming's mother, Xiaomei will not wait for Daming this time.

6   ___   Daming is afraid that Xiaomei will break up with him.

7   ___   Daming's mother thinks that Daming should find a different girlfriend through the Internet.

C   Read the passage, then mark the statements true or false. INTERPRETIVE

现在是电脑时代，网络对我们的生活越来越重要了。人们可以上网看新闻、查资料、和朋友聊天儿，还可以写博客，跟别人讨论有意思的问题。以前只能在图书馆查到的资料，现在可以很方便地在网上查到；以前只能在学校里学到的东西，现在可以很方便地从网上学到。这样下去，会不会有一天大家都觉得再也不用去图书馆，再也不用上大学了呢？要是世界上没有图书馆，也没有大学，我们的生活会怎么样呢？

現在是電腦時代，網絡對我們的生活越來越重要了。人們可以上網看新聞、查資料、和朋友聊天兒，還可以寫博客，跟別人討論有意思的問題。以前只能在圖書館查到的資料，現在可以很方便地在網上查到；以前只能在學校裡學到的東西，現在可以很方便地從網上學到。這樣下去，會不會有一天大家都覺得再也不用去圖書館，再也不用上大學了呢？要是世界上沒有圖書館，也沒有大學，我們的生活會怎麼樣呢？

1   ___   The writer is somewhat ambivalent about the changes that the Internet has brought to people's lives.

2   ___   The writer believes that the Internet is becoming increasingly important to people's lives.

3   ___   The writer is focused more on the academic than recreational use of the Internet.

4   ___   The writer appreciates the ease of acquiring information and knowledge on the Internet.

5   ___   The writer thinks that libraries are dispensable.

英语口语会话保证班
外企求职应聘技巧班
儿童资优口语班
电脑商务班

英語口語會話保證班
外企求職應聘技巧班
兒童資優口語班
電腦商務班

What courses are offered? List at least two.

_____

V. Writing and Grammar

A Form a character by combining the given components as indicated. Then use that character to write a word, phrase, or short sentence.

1 外边一个"门"，里边一个"耳"，
外邊一個"門"，裡邊一個"耳"，
是 _____ 的 _____。

2 上边一个"每次"的"次"，下边一个"贝"，
上邊一個"每次"的"次"，下邊一個"貝"，
是 _____ 的 _____。

3 左边一个人字旁，右边一个"五"，
左邊一個人字旁，右邊一個"五"，
是 _____ 的 _____。

4 左边一个"而且"的"且"，右边一个"力气"的"力"，
左邊一個"而且"的"且"，右邊一個"力氣"的"力"，
是 _____ 的 _____。

B Report how addicted the main characters are to their favorite activities, following the example below. **PRESENTATIONAL**

张天明玩儿电脑玩儿上瘾了，连吃饭的时候都上网。

張天明玩兒電腦玩兒上癮了，連吃飯的時候都上網。

1

2

3

4

Based on the Lesson Texts in Lessons 1–7, answer these questions. **INTERPERSONAL**

1 张天明的宿舍房间住得下住不下四个人？你怎么知道？

張天明的宿舍房間住得下住不下四個人？你怎麼知道？

_____

_____

2 张天明在学校附近吃得到吃不到地道的中国菜？你怎么知道？

張天明在學校附近吃得到吃不到地道的中國菜？你怎麼知道？

_____

_____

3 张天明离得开离不开网络？你怎么知道？

張天明離得開離不開網絡？你怎麼知道？

_____

_____

4 丽莎受得了受不了张天明老是迟到？你怎么知道？

麗莎受得了受不了張天明老是遲到？你怎麼知道？

_____

_____

D Based on the Lesson Texts in Lessons 1–7, use 结果/結果 to recap what the main characters end up doing, following the example below. PRESENTATIONAL

张天明跟李哲讨论选课的事，<u>结果决定选中文、经济和电脑课</u>。

张天明跟李哲討論選課的事，<u>結果決定選中文、經濟和電腦課</u>。

1 张天明去购物中心买衣服，_____。

张天明去購物中心買衣服，_____。

2 柯林说这个饭馆儿的鸡和鱼都做得不错，_____
_____。

柯林說這個飯館兒的雞和魚都做得不錯，_____
_____。

3 张天明知道在购物中心可以付现金，也可以用信用卡，他没带现金，_____。

张天明知道在購物中心可以付現金，也可以用信用卡，他没帶現金，_____。

4 张天明跟大家约好了一起去看电影，_____
_____。

張天明跟大家約好了一起去看電影，_____
_____。

E Fill in the blanks with either 或者 or 还是/還是. INTERPRETIVE

1 Q: 你爱吃广东菜 _____ 湖南菜？
   你愛吃廣東菜 _____ 湖南菜？

A: 广东菜 _____ 湖南菜，我都爱吃。
   廣東菜 _____ 湖南菜，我都愛吃。

2 学金融专业 _____ 电脑专业对将来找工作都很有帮
助。

学金融專業 _____ 電腦專業對將來找工作都很有幫
助。

3 网络对我们的生活无论有好处 _____ 有坏处，我们
都已经离不开网络了。

網絡對我們的生活無論有好處 _____ 有壞處，我們
都已經離不開網絡了。

F Translate these sentences into English. **INTERPRETIVE**

1 从去年十二月到今年八月，表姐都在电脑公司实习。
從去年十二月到今年八月，表姐都在電腦公司實習。

_____

2 从高中到大学，小李都在餐馆儿打工。
從高中到大學，小李都在餐館兒打工。

_____

3 从小到大，弟弟都不爱吃青菜。
從小到大，弟弟都不愛吃青菜。

_____

4 这家购物中心从一层到三层都在打折。
這家購物中心從一層到三層都在打折。

_____

5 从加州到纽约，坐飞机直飞差不多要五个多钟头。
從加州到紐約，坐飛機直飛差不多要五個多鐘頭。

_____

Fill in these blanks with the words or phrases given to form a coherent narrative. **INTERPRETIVE**

1　晚会

2　那天晚上

3　晚会快开完的时候

4　上个月25号

5　最后

6　在晚会上

＿＿＿＿＿＿＿＿＿＿＿＿＿＿，是我同屋的女朋友的生日。＿＿＿＿＿＿＿＿＿＿＿，在我们宿舍给她开了一个小小的生日晚会。＿＿＿＿＿＿＿＿＿＿八点半开始。＿＿＿＿＿＿＿＿＿＿＿＿，我们一边唱歌、聊天儿，一边吃东西。＿＿＿＿＿＿＿＿＿＿，我们吃蛋糕，大家玩儿得很高兴。＿＿＿＿＿＿＿＿＿＿＿＿，我同屋的女朋友对大家说："谢谢你们！"

1　晚會

2　那天晚上

3　晚會快開完的時候

4　上個月25號

5　最後

6　在晚會上

＿＿＿＿＿＿＿＿＿＿＿＿＿＿，是我同屋的女朋友的生日。＿＿＿＿＿＿＿＿＿＿＿，在我們宿舍給她開了一個小小的生日晚會。＿＿＿＿＿＿＿＿＿＿八點半開始。＿＿＿＿＿＿＿＿＿＿＿＿，我們一邊唱歌、聊天兒，一邊吃東西。＿＿＿＿＿＿＿＿＿＿，我們吃蛋糕，大家玩兒得很高興。＿＿＿＿＿＿＿＿＿＿＿＿，我同屋的女朋友對大家說："謝謝你們！"

H Translate these sentences into Chinese. **PRESENTATIONAL**

1　Comparing prices online is convenient. Online shopping is often tax free.

＿＿＿＿＿＿＿＿＿＿＿＿＿＿＿＿＿＿＿＿＿＿＿＿＿＿＿＿＿＿＿＿＿

2　The articles in this magazine are all garbage. Stop reading them!

＿＿＿＿＿＿＿＿＿＿＿＿＿＿＿＿＿＿＿＿＿＿＿＿＿＿＿＿＿＿＿＿＿

3　My uncle doesn't know how to send WeChat messages, send emails, or go online. He is so behind the times.

＿＿＿＿＿＿＿＿＿＿＿＿＿＿＿＿＿＿＿＿＿＿＿＿＿＿＿＿＿＿＿＿＿

4　I'll be done writing my article soon. Thank you for helping me with the translation.

＿＿＿＿＿＿＿＿＿＿＿＿＿＿＿＿＿＿＿＿＿＿＿＿＿＿＿＿＿＿＿＿＿

I Translate these dialogues into Chinese. PRESENTATIONAL

1 **Person A:** Hello, is this the school computer center? My computer is broken.

_____

_____

Person B: What's wrong?

_____

Person A: Yesterday I downloaded a program. Just now I was writing an article and, at the same time, looking for references online. But I don't know why my computer just broke—and it ended up that the article I was writing disappeared, too.

_____

_____

_____

_____

Person B: Although the world of the Internet is vast and very convenient, and you can find whatever reference materials, if you're careless, you can bring problems on yourself.

_____

_____

_____

Person A: Then what do I do?

_____

Person B: Please bring your computer to the school computer center. We can help you take a look.

_____

Person A: Thank you. I'll be right there.

_____

2 Lisha: Xuemei, Tianming spends so much time on his computer. His computer is on from morning till night.

_____

_____

Xuemei: It's the era of the Internet now. You cannot be without a computer.

_____

Lisha: When he's online, he doesn't take a break for one moment. He seems to have become addicted.

_____

_____

Xuemei: Is it as serious as that?

_____

_____

J Translate these passages into Chinese. PRESENTATIONAL

1 How convenient it is in the era of the Internet. You can buy things, make friends, and find information online. Some people write blogs on their own websites. There are also many people who like to chat online. There is a whole other world online. The Internet has made the world even bigger. Or you could say the Internet has made the world even smaller.

_____

_____

_____

_____

_____

_____

2　Do you have your own website? Do you blog? Do you often forget the time once you go online? Is your computer on from morning till night? Do you shop, order takeout, read the news, and check references? If you say "yes" to all, then you are probably addicted!

_____

_____

_____

_____

_____

_____

3　Zhang Tianming's blog:
Starting tomorrow, I probably won't be able to write my blog every day because my girlfriend says I'm online all day, and she cannot take it anymore. She is going to break up with me if I don't spend more time with her. This is serious. Don't assume she is joking. She sounds like she's truly angry. I love blogging, but I love my girlfriend more.

_____

_____

_____

_____

_____

_____

K List your online activities in Chinese and rank them based on how frequently you do them or how important they are to your daily life. PRESENTATIONAL

1 _____

2 _____

3 _____

4 _____

5 _____

6 _____

7 _____

L Pick one thing you do online and explain in Chinese why it's essential to your daily life, the impact it has on you, and why you cannot live without it. PRESENTATIONAL

M Pick one thing you do online that you wish you could give up. Explain in Chinese whether you are addicted to it, and why you want to cut down or quit. If applicable, provide alternatives to replace it. PRESENTATIONAL

N You plan to send in a ninety-second video resume to go with your job application to an international company in China. Before shooting the video, draft a script. Include basic information such as your name, background, education, skills, and work experience, and discuss why your personal traits make you suitable for the job. PRESENTATIONAL

O Write a story in Chinese based on the four images below. Make sure that your story has a beginning, middle, and end, and that the transition from one picture to the next is smooth and logical. **PRESENTATIONAL**

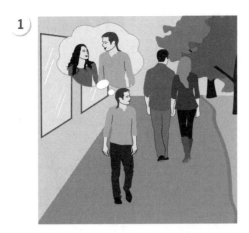

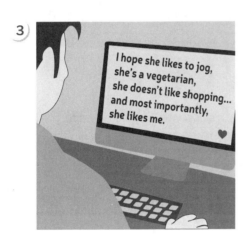

_____

_____

_____

_____

_____

Lesson 8

第八课

第八課

打工
Working Part-Time

 Check off the following language functions as you learn how to:

- [ ] Explain how people fund their education
- [ ] Discuss if you work part-time and why
- [ ] Name common jobs for students
- [ ] Talk about how students spend their pocket money

As you progress through the lesson, note other language functions you would like to learn.

_____

_____

_____

I. Listening Comprehension

A Listen to the Lesson Text audio, then circle the most appropriate choice. INTERPRETIVE

1 What has helped Zhang Tianming's parents pay for their son's and daughter's college education?

   a   a loan

   b   long-term savings

   c   both of the above

2 Why has Zhang Tianming decided to look for a job?

   a   to gain experience and reduce financial pressure on his parents

   b   to reduce financial pressure on his parents and make more friends

   c   to make more friends and gain experience

3 How does Lisha pay for her tuition?

   a   with a loan

   b   with a scholarship

   c   both of the above

4 Who do restaurants in China prefer to hire for their waitstaff?

   a   unemployed people in the city

   b   people from the countryside

   c   college students

5 What problem does Lisha's roommate have?

   a   She doesn't like the food at the student cafeteria.

   b   She doesn't get enough money from her parents.

   c   She spends too freely.

B Listen to the Workbook Dialogue audio, then mark these statements true or false. INTERPRETIVE

1 _____ The speakers are most likely a student and a professor.

2 _____ The man has been working for about a month.

3 _____ The man does not work all day on Wednesday.

4 _____ By making some money, the man has reduced the burden on the woman.

C Based on the Workbook Dialogue audio, circle the most appropriate choice. INTERPRETIVE

1 How much did the man make last month?

   a $100

   b $400

   c $500

2 At the end of the dialogue, how does the woman most likely feel?

a disappointed

b happy

c indifferent

D Listen to the Workbook Narrative 1 audio, then mark these statements true or false. INTERPRETIVE

1 ____ Chinese parents typically place much importance on their children's education.

2 ____ Many rural parents move to the cities to be close to their college-going children.

3 ____ Rural parents discourage their college-going children from working part-time because they want their children to concentrate on their studies.

E Listen to the Workbook Narrative 2 audio, then circle the most appropriate choice. INTERPRETIVE

1 In the past, Chinese college students had to pay for

a tuition but not living expenses.

b living expenses but not tuition.

c neither tuition nor living expenses.

2 Today, parents of Chinese college students have to pay for

a their children's tuition and living expenses.

b their children's tuition but not their living expenses.

c their children's living expenses but not their tuition.

3 By working part-time, students can

a pay for their tuition themselves.

b pay for their living expenses themselves.

c make some pocket money for themselves.

F Listen to the Workbook Narrative 3 audio, then circle the most appropriate choice. INTERPRETIVE

1 Little Bai's parents don't pay for his tuition because

a Little Bai pays for it himself.

b Little Bai pays for it with a loan.

c Little Bai pays for it with a scholarship.

2 How much money do Little Bai's parents give him each month?

a $1,000

b $800

c $500

3 Little Bai worked

a first as a translator and later as a waiter.

b first as a waiter and later as a translator.

c first as a tutor and later as a translator.

4 How much money does Little Bai expect from his parents next month?

  a $0

  b $300

  c $500

G _____ Listen to the Workbook Listening Rejoinder audio. After hearing the first speaker, select the best response from the four choices given by the second speaker. Indicate the letter of your choice. INTERPRETIVE

II. Pinyin and Tone

A Compare the pronunciations of the underlined characters in the two words/phrases given. Provide their initials in *pinyin*.

减<u>轻</u>/减<u>輕</u> _____   <u>经</u>验/<u>經</u>驗 _____

B Compare the tones of the underlined characters in the two words/phrases given. Indicate the tones with 1 (first tone), 2 (second tone), 3 (third tone), 4 (fourth tone), or 0 (neutral tone).

<u>留</u>学生/<u>留</u>學生 _____   <u>遛</u>狗 _____

III. Speaking

A Practice asking and answering these questions. INTERPERSONAL

1 你一边上学一边打工吗？为什么？

  你一邊上學一邊打工嗎？為什麼？

2 你觉得自己的经济压力大不大？

  你覺得自己的經濟壓力大不大？

3 你觉得爸爸妈妈的经济负担重不重？

  你覺得爸爸媽媽的經濟負擔重不重？

4 你怎么付学费？父母帮助，自己挣钱，申请奖学金，
还是跟政府贷款？

你怎麼付學費？父母幫助，自己掙錢，申請獎學金，
還是跟政府貸款？

5 你一般怎么吃饭？自己做，叫外卖，还是在学生餐厅吃？

你一般怎麼吃飯？自己做，叫外賣，還是在學生餐廳吃？

B Practice speaking with these prompts. PRESENTATIONAL

1 请谈谈一边上学一边打工对学习有什么影响。

請談談一邊上學一邊打工對學習有什麼影響。

2 请谈谈孩子怎么样可以减轻父母的经济负担。

請談談孩子怎麼樣可以減輕父母的經濟負擔。

3 You are trying to persuade your parents to allow you to work part-time while in school. In Chinese, provide reasons to support your request and convince them that you will be both academically and financially responsible.

IV. Reading Comprehension

A Complete this section by writing the characters, *pinyin*, and English equivalent of each new word formed. Guess the meaning, then use a dictionary to confirm.

1 "收入"的"入"+"门口"的"口"

"收入"的"入"+"門口"的"口"

→ 入 ＋ 口→ _____ _____ _____

2 "身体"的"体"+"教育"的"育"

"身體"的"體"+"教育"的"育"

→ 体/體 ＋ 育→ _____ _____ _____

3 "存钱"的"存"+"菜单"的"单"

  "存錢"的"存"+"菜單"的"單"

  → 存 + 单/單→ _____ _____ _____

4 "零用钱"的"零"+"衣食住行"的"食"

  "零用錢"的"零"+"衣食住行"的"食"

  → 零 + 食→ _____ _____ _____

5 "工资"的"资"+"现金"的"金"

  "工資"的"資"+"現金"的"金"

  → 资/資 + 金→ _____ _____ _____

B This is an email sent from the provost's office to all students at a Chinese college. Read the message, then mark the statements true or false. INTERPRETIVE

开学已经一个星期了，可是有一些同学还没有回到学校。我们给他们的家长打电话，才知道他们在给旅行社当导游或翻译，还没回来。学校觉得同学们打工，取得工作经验，是好事。可是你们的学习比打工挣钱更重要。我们知道，你们的学费和生活费对很多父母来说压力不小，学校也在想办法减轻你们的经济负担，但是因为打工不上课是不对的。而且，如果因为打工影响了学习，应该毕业的时候不能毕业，会让你们父母的经济负担更重。我们希望大家别为了打工忘了学习。

開學已經一個星期了，可是有一些同學還沒有回到學校。我們給他們的家長打電話，才知道他們在給旅行社當導遊或翻譯，還沒回來。學校覺得同學們打工，取得工作經驗，是好事。可是你們的學習比打工掙錢更重要。我們知道，你們的學費和生活費對很多父母來說壓力不小，學校也在想辦法減輕你們的經濟負擔，但是因為打工不上課是不對的。而且，如果因為打工影響了學習，應該畢業的時候不能畢業，會讓你們父母的經濟負擔更重。我們希望大家別為了打工忘了學習。

1 ___ The students who are not yet back at school are still out of town.

2 ___ This email sounds sympathetic to students' families' financial difficulties.

3 ___ The provost's office promises to cut tuition fees and living expenses.

4 ___ According to the email, it can make things worse for parents if a student spends too much time working.

5 ___ The provost's office prohibits students from working during the semester.

C Read the following email, then mark the statements true or false. INTERPRETIVE

爸爸：

　　您给我寄来的这个月的生活费收到了，九百块，比上个月又多了五十块。我上个月的生活费还没用完，这个月您给我寄六百块就够了。您在餐馆儿工作那么累，工资又低，挣钱多不容易啊。每次想到这儿我就想哭。我们班有个叫毛毛的男同学，因为他爸爸有自己的公司非常有钱，就乱花钱，每天不是上饭馆儿，就是唱卡拉OK，每个月他爸爸都要给他好几千块钱。我觉得他们心里除了钱还是钱。我的爸爸比他们棒多了，因为您教给了我很多学校里学不到的东西。

丽丽

爸爸：

　　您給我寄來的這個月的生活費收到了，九百塊，比上個月又多了五十塊。我上個月的生活費還沒用完，這個月您給我寄六百塊就夠了。您在餐館兒工作那麼累，工資又低，掙錢多不容易啊。每次想到這兒我就想哭。我們班有個叫毛毛的男同學，因為他爸爸有自己的公司非常有錢，就亂花錢，每天不是上飯館兒，就是唱卡拉OK，每個月他爸爸都要給他好幾千塊錢。我覺得他們心裡除了錢還是錢。我的爸爸比他們棒多了，因為您教給了我很多學校裡學不到的東西。

麗麗

1 ____ Lili's monthly allowance has been increased.

2 ____ Lili's father owns a restaurant.

3 ____ Every time Lili is out of money, she wants to cry.

4 ____ Maomao covers his expenses on his own by working at his father's company.

5 ____ Lili is proud of her father because he never fails to send her money.

6 ____ Lili is a frugal and considerate daughter.

D Look at the poster, then answer the questions in English. INTERPRETIVE

值班经理：4000－5000元

制作员： 3500－4500元

服务员： 2000－3000元

接待员： 2000－2500元

洗碗工： 2000－2500元

以上人员均提供食宿。

本店常年招聘小时工。

有意者请内洽值班经理。

值班經理：4000－5000元

製作員： 3500－4500元

服務員： 2000－3000元

接待員： 2000－2500元

洗碗工： 2000－2500元

以上人員均提供食宿。

本店常年招聘小時工。

有意者請內洽值班經理。

1 What positions are they trying to fill? List two positions.

_____

2 Would you be interested in applying for any of the positions advertised? Why?

_____

3 What benefits are offered in addition to a basic salary?

_____

Look at this ad, then answer the questions in Chinese. **INTERPERSONAL**

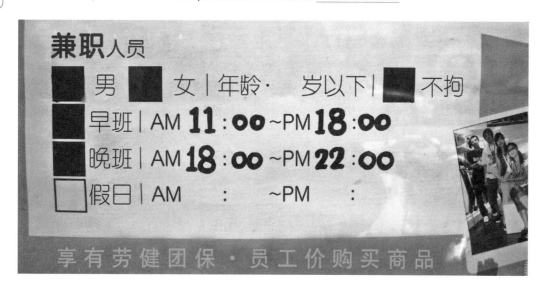

1 广告中的"早班"和"晚班"是什么意思?

廣告中的"早班"和"晚班"是什麼意思?

2 你会申请这份工作吗?为什么?

你會申請這份工作嗎?為什麼?

Look at this form, then complete the tasks in English. **INTERPRETIVE**

中国工商银行北京市分行 缴费申请单

			年　　月　　日
缴　费 种　类	☐　移动话费 ☐　电　费	☐　市话费 ☐　收视费	☐　上网费 ☐　其他
单位代码		用户代码	
缴费金额 或 购电度数		用户姓名	

为保证准确受理您的缴费业务，请协助填写以上内容。

中國工商銀行北京市分行 缴费申请单

			年　　月　　日
缴　费 種　類	☐　移動話費 ☐　電　費	☐　市話費 ☐　收視費	☐　上網費 ☐　其他
單位代碼		用户代碼	
缴费金額 或 購電度數		用户姓名	

為保證準確受理您的缴費業務，請協助填寫以上內容。

1 Circle the name of the bank.

2 What fees does the form allow to be deducted directly from your account? List at least two.

_____

3 Sign and date the slip.

A Form a character by combining the given components as indicated. Then use that character to write a word, phrase, or short sentence.

1 左边一个人字旁，右边一个"一共"的"共"，

   左邊一個人字旁，右邊一個"一共"的"共"，

   是 _____ 的 _____。

2 左边一个"耳"，右边一个"又"，

   左邊一個"耳"，右邊一個"又"，

   是 _____ 的 _____。

3 上边一个"将来"的"将"，下边一个"大"，

   上邊一個"將來"的"將"，下邊一個"大"，

   是 _____ 的 _____。

4 左边一个言字旁，右边一个"卖东西"的"卖"，

   左邊一個言字旁，右邊一個"賣東西"的"賣"，

   是 _____ 的 _____。

B Draw lines to connect each verb with an object. INTERPRETIVE

申请／申請　　　　　　　负担／負擔

受到　　　　　　　　　　生活

减轻／減輕　　　　　　　问题／問題

取得　　　　　　　　　　工作

解决／解決　　　　　　　影响／影響

适应／適應　　　　　　　经验／經驗

C Read this dialogue, then fill in the blanks with the phrases provided. INTERPRETIVE

想出来   省下来   说出来   看出来

Person A: 我 _____ 你心里有事。怎么了？有什么事儿，
_____ 听听。说不定我能帮忙。

Person B: 最近经济不好，我父母都没有工作。为了减轻
父母的经济负担，我从学校宿舍搬回家住，把
饭钱、住宿费都 _____，但家里的生活费还是
问题。

Person A: 别着急。办法是人 _____ 的。……对了，我们
公司正好在找英文翻译，你可以试试。

Person B: 是吗？那我明天就去申请。

想出來   省下來   說出來   看出來

Person A: 我 _____ 你心裡有事。怎麼了？有什麼事兒，
_____ 聽聽。說不定我能幫忙。

Person B: 最近經濟不好，我父母都沒有工作。為了減輕
父母的經濟負擔，我從學校宿舍搬回家住，把
飯錢、住宿費都 _____，但家裡的生活費還是
問題。

Person A: 別著急。辦法是人 _____ 的。……對了，我們
公司正好在找英文翻譯，你可以試試。

Person B: 是嗎？那我明天就去申請。

D Fill in the blanks with 适合/適合 or 合适/合適. INTERPRETIVE

1 小王喜欢查资料，这份研究工作对他很 ____。

   小王喜歡查資料，這份研究工作對他很 ____。

2 你不爱跟小孩打交道，不____ 做家教。

   你不愛跟小孩打交道，不____ 做家教。

3 他病了好几天，我们应该去看看他。只是发微信、打
手机，我觉得不____。

   他病了好幾天，我們應該去看看他。只是發微信、打
手機，我覺得不____。

4 这条牛仔裤长短 ____ ，样子、颜色也不错，很 ____ 你。

这條牛仔褲長短 ____ ，樣子、顏色也不錯，很 ____ 你。

5 他们两个文化背景、教育背景都不同，在一起不 ____ 。

他們兩個文化背景、教育背景都不同，在一起不 ____ 。

6 我对猫和狗过敏，所以不 ____ 帮别人喂猫遛狗。

我對貓和狗過敏，所以不 ____ 幫別人餵貓遛狗。

E Based on these illustrations, describe people's routines using 不是…， 就是…, following the example below. PRESENTATIONAL

Teacher Li   every Saturday

李老师每个星期六不是洗衣服，就是打扫房间。

李老師每個星期六不是洗衣服，就是打掃房間。

1 Zhang Tianming's father   every night

_____

2    when riding the bus

_____

3    when shopping for meat

_____

我去年寒假去纽约看我哥哥。
我12月16号从这里坐飞机去纽约。
我在飞机上坐在一个女孩儿旁边。
那个女孩儿很漂亮。
开始我不好意思跟她说话。
那个女孩儿要写字。
她没带笔。
我很高兴地把我的笔给她。
她写完字我们开始聊天儿。
我们聊天儿聊得很高兴。
快下飞机了，她告诉了我她的电话号码。
我说一定给她打电话。

我去年寒假去紐約看我哥哥。
我12月16號從這裡坐飛機去紐約。
我在飛機上坐在一個女孩兒旁邊。
那個女孩兒很漂亮。
開始我不好意思跟她說話。
那個女孩兒要寫字。
她沒帶筆。
我很高興地把我的筆給她。
她寫完字我們開始聊天兒。
我們聊天兒聊得很高興。
快下飛機了，她告訴了我她的電話號碼。
我說一定給她打電話。

_____

_____

_____

_____

_____

_____

_____

_____

_____

_____

_____

G Translate these sentences into Chinese. PRESENTATIONAL

1 I am all grown up. I should start making money to lessen my parents' financial burden.

_____

2 The professor suggested that we go online to read Chinese newspapers in order to improve our Chinese.

_____

3 On weekends, he stays in his room all day. If he's not blogging, he's sleeping.

_____

4 No one can stand going shopping with him. If he's not complaining that the quality is poor, he's complaining that the prices are too expensive.

_____

_____

Translate these dialogues into Chinese. PRESENTATIONAL

1 **Person A:** Why do you want to get a part-time job?

_____

Person B: I'd like to make some spending money. If I earn the money myself, I can spend it however I want. It's liberating and I can ease my parents' burden at the same time.

_____

_____

Person A: Do you have time to work? Will it affect your studies?

_____

Person B: I'd like to work over summer break. It won't affect my studies.

_____

Person A: Where do you want to work?

_____

Person B: I plan to go to medical school later, so I'd like to get a job at a hospital to see whether I like dealing with patients. What about you?

_____

_____

Person A: I'd like to take classes in the summer.

_____

2 **Person A:** I spent too much money this semester and now I have a lot of credit card debt.

_____

Person B: Then what do you plan to do?

_____

Person A: I haven't come up with a solution. I can only pay (it) back slowly.

Person B: Then borrow some money from your parents.

Person A: They're under financial pressure, too. I would be embarrassed to borrow money from them.

Person B: I'm working as a tutor. You can also tutor or work in computer maintenance.

Person A: I'm not suited to being a tutor, but I can maintain computers.

I Translate this advertisement into Chinese. PRESENTATIONAL

Do you want to make money? Do you want to gain work experience? Do you know how to speak English? Do you know how to use a computer? Do you want to be a tutor? We are a tutoring center and have many tutoring jobs. If you are interested, you can start applying right away. You don't need to be experienced. We will teach you how to be a tutor, but you must like dealing with children. If you have any questions, please check out our website or send us a WeChat message.

Translate these email messages into Chinese. **PRESENTATIONAL**

1 Wenwen (文文),

Your dad and I hope that you won't work this summer. You can take some classes. If you have enough credits, you can graduate early and pay back the government loan earlier. If you don't want to take classes, you can relax a bit. If you need pocket money, you can borrow it from us. We know that you are a good daughter and you want to lessen our financial burden. But your sister has already graduated from college, so we don't have to pay for her tuition or living expenses anymore. Our burden is not as heavy as it used to be. Don't worry.

Mom

_____

_____

_____

_____

_____

_____

_____

2 Mom,

I don't need to borrow money from you and Dad. I've saved up some money this year. I don't owe the bank or my credit card company any money, so I'm not under any financial pressure. Summer break is long, so I can take one class and work after finishing the class. I want to work, not just to make money. Gaining some work experience is also important. I'll also have time to have fun. Sis and I agreed to travel to China before school starts. Her college roommate now works at a bank in Beijing. She's willing to be our tour guide. I have a Chinese test this afternoon. I have to review now. I'll call you this weekend.

Wenwen

_____

_____

_____

_____

_____

_____

_____

K Imagine that you're a financial advisor. You're compiling a useful resource for Chinese students who'd like to be smart about spending and saving. PRESENTATIONAL

First, compile a list of common spending problems:

_____

_____

_____

_____

Second, provide a list of financial dos and don'ts to help build a healthy financial future:

Do:	Don't:
_____	_____
_____	_____
_____	_____
_____	_____

L Write a story in Chinese based on the four images below. Make sure that your story has a beginning, middle, and end, and that the transition from one picture to the next is smooth and logical. PRESENTATIONAL

_____

_____

_____

_____

_____

教育
Education

 Check off the following language functions as you learn how to:

〔 〕 Name some typical classes offered in afterschool programs

〔 〕 State whether you agree or disagree with others' points of view

〔 〕 Present your opinions on children's education

〔 〕 Discuss parents' hopes and expectations for their children

As you progress through the lesson, note other language functions you would like to learn.

_____

_____

_____

A Listen to the Lesson Text audio, then circle the most appropriate choice. INTERPRETIVE

1 **What do Li Zhe's brother and sister-in-law argue about?**

a website design and management

b family finances

c their daughter's education

2 **What does Li Zhe's niece complain to Li Zhe about?**

a her busy schedule

b her parents' arguments

c her parents' busy schedules

3 **On which day of the week is Li Zhe's niece least busy?**

a Thursday

b Friday

c Saturday

4 **What does Lisha think about Li Zhe's sister-in-law's approach to her daughter's education?**

a She completely agrees with it.

b She understands but does not completely agree with it.

c She completely disagrees with it.

5 **Why does Lisha say that Li Zhe has become a "philosopher"?**

a Because he has taken courses in philosophy.

b Because he has been reading a lot of philosophy.

c Because he talks like a philosopher.

B Listen to the Workbook Dialogue audio, then mark these statements true or false. INTERPRETIVE

1 ____ The speakers are most likely husband and wife.

2 ____ Xiaoming is most likely the man's son or daughter.

3 ____ Xiaoming has complained to the woman about the man.

4 ____ Xiaoming enjoys his piano lessons but not his swimming lessons.

5 ____ The man believes that children must be put under some pressure in order to succeed in the future.

6 ____ The man didn't become a good lawyer because he wasn't pushed to learn many things as a child.

C   Listen to the Workbook Narrative 1 audio, then mark these statements true or false. INTERPRETIVE

1 ____   **Little Qian liked his new job at the beginning.**

2 ____   **The students' parents called Little Qian for opposite reasons.**

3 ____   **Little Qian realizes he was overly demanding of his students.**

4 ____   **Little Qian is pleased with the phone calls.**

D   Listen to the Workbook Narrative 2 audio, then circle the most appropriate choice. INTERPRETIVE

1   **What are Anthony's parents interested in?**

   a   His father is interested in sports, and his mother in music.

   b   His father is interested in music, and his mother in sports.

   c   His parents are both interested in music and sports.

2   **Anthony's parents agree that he should take**

   a   swimming lessons.

   b   piano lessons.

   c   nothing.

3   **Which of his parents' interests does Anthony share?**

   a   swimming

   b   piano

   c   neither of the above

E   Listen to the Workbook Narrative 3 audio, then circle the most appropriate choice. INTERPRETIVE

1   **The speaker is**

   a   a teacher.

   b   a student.

   c   a student's parent.

2   **Who is the speaker addressing?**

   a   teachers

   b   students

   c   students' parents

3   **According to the speaker, the school has a problem with**

   a   absenteeism.

   b   too many extracurricular activities.

   c   too few extracurricular activities.

4   **According to the speaker, most of the pressure on children comes from**

   a   teachers.

   b   parents.

   c   the children themselves.

_____ Listen to the Workbook Listening Rejoinder audio. After hearing the first speaker, select the best response from the four choices given by the second speaker. Indicate the letter of your choice. INTERPRETIVE

II. Pinyin and Tone

A Compare the pronunciations of the underlined characters in the two words or phrases given. Provide their initials in *pinyin*.

设<u>计</u>/設<u>計</u> _____   硕<u>士</u>/碩<u>士</u> _____

B Compare the tones of the underlined characters in the two words or phrases given. Indicate the tones with 1 (first tone), 2 (second tone), 3 (third tone), 4 (fourth tone), or 0 (neutral tone).

<u>为</u>什么/<u>為</u>什麼 _____   认<u>为</u>/認<u>為</u> _____

III. Speaking

A Practice asking and answering these questions. INTERPERSONAL

1 你小时候学过钢琴、画画儿、游泳吗？

你小時候學過鋼琴、畫畫兒、游泳嗎？

2 如果学过，学了多长时间？是你自己想学的，还是父母
要你学的？

如果學過，學了多長時間？是你自己想學的，還是父母
要你學的？

3 你童年的时候学习压力大不大？有没有时间玩儿？

你童年的時候學習壓力大不大？有沒有時間玩兒？

1 请谈谈如果学习压力很大，你怎么让自己轻松一些。

请谈谈如果學習壓力很大，你怎麼讓自己輕鬆一些。

2 请谈谈你理解不理解父母下课以后或周末送孩子学这学那的做法。

請談談你理解不理解父母下課以後或週末送孩子學這學那的做法。

3 Suppose you could relive your childhood. Express in Chinese what you wish your parents and/or you had done differently in terms of your schoolwork and extracurricular activities.

IV. Reading Comprehension

A Complete this section by writing the characters, *pinyin*, and English equivalent of each new word formed. Guess the meaning, then use a dictionary to confirm.

1 "安排"的"排"+"球迷"的"球"

"安排"的"排"+"球迷"的"球"

→ 排 + 球→ _____ _____ _____

2 "抱怨"的"怨"+"生气"的"气"

"抱怨"的"怨"+"生氣"的"氣"

→ 怨 + 气/氣→ _____ _____ _____

3 "学校"的"校"+"家长"的"长"

"學校"的"校"+"家長"的"長"

→ 校 + 长/長→ _____ _____ _____

4 "口味"的"口"+"钢琴"的"琴"

　"口味"的"口"+"鋼琴"的"琴"

　→ 口 + 琴→ ＿＿＿＿ ＿＿＿＿ ＿＿＿＿

5 "农村"的"农"+"事业"的"业"

　"農村"的"農"+"事業"的"業"

　→ 农/農 + 业/業→ ＿＿＿＿ ＿＿＿＿ ＿＿＿＿

B Read the conversation, then mark the statements true or false. INTERPRETIVE

柯林： 雪梅，你钢琴弹得棒极了！你是几岁开始学的钢琴？

雪梅： 四岁。

柯林： 你怎么四岁就开始对钢琴有兴趣了？

雪梅： 我四岁的时候没见过几次钢琴，怎么会有兴趣？我妈妈开始带我上钢琴学校的时候，我一看见钢琴就哭。可是妈妈一定要上完课才带我回家。

柯林： 她怎么能让你学你没有兴趣的东西呢？

雪梅： 我妈妈有她的道理。她说，学钢琴要早，等到孩子自己对钢琴有兴趣，可能就太晚了。

柯林： 有道理。我十岁的时候开始喜欢钢琴，后来也学了好几年，可是现在跟你比，差得太多了。

雪梅： 我的爱好和兴趣是妈妈帮我选择的。一开始我常常抱怨，可是后来我就真的喜欢钢琴了，越学越轻松，越学越快乐。

柯林： 现在我开始理解像你妈妈那样的中国父母教育孩子的做法了。

柯林：雪梅，你鋼琴彈得棒極了！你是幾歲開始
　　　學的鋼琴？

雪梅：四歲。

柯林：你怎麼四歲就開始對鋼琴有興趣了？

雪梅：我四歲的時候沒見過幾次鋼琴，怎麼會有興
　　　趣？我媽媽開始帶我上鋼琴學校的時候，我
　　　一看見鋼琴就哭。可是媽媽一定要上完課才
　　　帶我回家。

柯林：她怎麼能讓你學你沒有興趣的東西呢？

雪梅：我媽媽有她的道理。她說，學鋼琴要早，等
　　　到孩子自己對鋼琴有興趣，可能就太晚了。

柯林：有道理。我十歲的時候開始喜歡鋼琴，後
　　　來也學了好幾年，可是現在跟你比，差得
　　　太多了。

雪梅：我的愛好和興趣是媽媽幫我選擇的。一開
　　　始我常常抱怨，可是後來我就真的喜歡鋼
　　　琴了，越學越輕鬆，越學越快樂。

柯林：現在我開始理解像你媽媽那樣的中國父母
　　　教育孩子的做法了。

1 ＿＿ Xuemei was uninterested in the piano when she began taking lessons.

2 ＿＿ Xuemei often cried when her mother took her home from piano school.

3 ＿＿ Xuemei's mother insisted that children should start taking piano lessons early.

4 ＿＿ Ke Lin's parents made him take piano lessons when he was ten.

5 ＿＿ According to Ke Lin, Xuemei plays the piano better than he does.

6 ＿＿ Xuemei sounds quite grateful that her mother made her take piano lessons when she was young.

7 ＿＿ Ke Lin has always been sympathetic to Xuemei's mother's ideas about children's education.

Read the passage, then mark the statements true or false. Note: 虫／蟲 (chóng) means "insect" or "bug." **INTERPRETIVE**

在中国，很多父母都希望自己的孩子学的东西越多越好，这样孩子长大了才能做出一番大事业。因为有这种望子成龙望女成凤的想法，所以很多家长让孩子学这学那，不太考虑孩子自己的兴趣和爱好。有的孩子因为太忙，休息不够，影响了身体健康。还有的孩子因为压力太大，没有时间跟其它小朋友一起玩儿，所以觉得自己的童年不快乐。北京有个十二岁的男孩儿说："爸爸妈妈一直希望我长大了成为一条龙。可是我不愿意当一条不快乐的龙，只愿意当一条快乐的虫 (chóng)。"

在中國，很多父母都希望自己的孩子學的東西越多越好，這樣孩子長大了才能做出一番大事業。因為有這種望子成龍望女成鳳的想法，所以很多家長讓孩子學這學那，不太考慮孩子自己的興趣和愛好。有的孩子因為太忙，休息不夠，影響了身體健康。還有的孩子因為壓力太大，沒有時間跟其他小朋友一起玩兒，所以覺得自己的童年不快樂。北京有個十二歲的男孩兒說："爸爸媽媽一直希望我長大了成為一條龍。可是我不願意當一條不快樂的龍，只願意當一條快樂的蟲 (chóng)。"

1 ____ The author asserts that many Chinese parents have very high expectations for their children.

2 ____ Some children in China are overly busy because they are interested in too many things.

3 ____ The author believes that when children are too busy, it can be detrimental to their health.

4 ____ Some children have to be pressured into spending time playing with their friends.

5 ____ The twelve-year-old boy fully understands his parents' efforts to make him study harder.

6 ____ The author disapproves of forcing children to learn many things.

D Look at this newspaper advertisement, then answer the questions in English. INTERPRETIVE

同学家教服务社
专教：高国中小
　　英数理化
电子学，会计，电脑
儿童英语，钢琴
经验丰富到府任教

同學家教服務社
專教：高國中小
　　英數理化
電子學，會計，電腦
兒童英語，鋼琴
經驗豐富到府任教

1　What classes can parents sign their children up for? List at least three.

_____

2　Does the ad target elementary, junior high, or high school students? How do you know?

_____

3　Circle the words that mean "tutorial services."

E Look at this newspaper advertisement, then answer the questions in English. INTERPRETIVE

小初高 教师1对1
暑假轻松自在提成绩，上学大教育！
一线教师1对1面授
授课陪读答疑3种教学模式
知识 习惯 方法 3方面提高

小初高教师1對1
暑假輕鬆自在提成績，上學大教育！
一線教師1對1面授
授課陪讀答疑3種教學模式
知識 習慣 方法 3方面提高

1　What's the student-teacher ratio?

_____

2　What time of year does this advertisement encourage people to sign up for classes?

_____

3　In which areas does the advertisement guarantee good results? Name at least one.

_____

A Form a character by combining the given components as indicated. Then use that character to write a word, phrase, or short sentence.

1 左边一个"禾"，右边一个"多"，

  左邊一個"禾"，右邊一個"多"，

  是 _____ 的 _____。

2 左边一个提手旁，右边一个"非常"的"非"，

  左邊一個提手旁，右邊一個"非常"的"非"，

  是 _____ 的 _____。

3 上边两个"王"，下边一个"今天"的"今"，

  上邊兩個"王"，下邊一個"今天"的"今"，

  是 _____ 的 _____。

4 左边一个示字旁，右边一个"土"，

  左邊一個示字旁，右邊一個"土"，

  是 _____ 的 _____。

B Fill in the blanks with 的, 得, or 地. **INTERPRETIVE**

　　我们两个相处_____那么好，我理解你_____想法，你同意我_____看法，我一直以为你是我_____好朋友。可是没想到为了借钱，我们吵架吵_____那么厉害。到底什么重要？钱还是朋友？我们应该好好儿_____想想。

　　我們兩個相處_____那麼好，我理解你_____想法，你同意我_____看法，我一直以為你是我_____好朋友。可是沒想到為了借錢，我們吵架吵_____那麼厲害。到底什麼重要？錢還是朋友？我們應該好好兒_____想想。

C Reply to these statements to set the record straight, using 不是⋯，而是⋯, following the example below. **INTERPERSONAL**

Q: 林雪梅是从上海来的吧?
林雪梅是從上海來的吧？

A: 林雪梅不是从上海来的，而是从杭州来的。
林雪梅不是從上海來的，而是從杭州來的。

1 Q: 林雪梅爱吃辣的吧?
林雪梅愛吃辣的吧？

A: _____

2 Q: 张天明下个学期好像选了金融课。
張天明下個學期好像選了金融課。

A: _____

3 Q: 丽莎对球赛很有兴趣吧?
麗莎對球賽很有興趣吧？

A: _____

4 Q: 听说丽莎不让张天明上网?
聽說麗莎不讓張天明上網？

A: _____

5 Q: 丽莎好像同意李哲嫂子的做法吧?
麗莎好像同意李哲嫂子的做法吧？

A: _____

Practice asking and answering questions based on the topics, following the example below.
INTERPERSONAL

children	study	VS.	have fun	important

Q: 你认为小孩子学习重要还是玩儿重要？
　　你認為小孩子學習重要還是玩兒重要？

A: 我认为小孩子（your choice）重要。
　　我認為小孩子（your choice）重要。

1 Li Zhe　　　　find a job　　　VS.　　go to graduate school　good

Q: _____

A: _____

2 Zhang Tianming　live on campus　VS.　　live off campus　　convenient

Q: _____

A: _____

3 Zhang Tianming　study literature　VS.　　study finance　　appropriate

Q: _____

A: _____

4 Lin Xuemei　　study　　　　　VS.　　date　　　　　important

Q: _____

A: _____

E Fill in the blanks with the given words and phrases to form a coherent narrative. INTERPRETIVE

1 结果	5 可是	9 昨天
2 我	6 所以	10 在那里
3 虽然	7 后来	
4 可是	8 今天早上	

_____我在网上看见学校附近的购物中心有很多商店在打折。_____起床后我就开车去那个购物中心。_____，很多商店真的都打折，我很高兴。_____想买一套运动服，_____走进了一家卖运动服的商店。进去一看，什么都打六折，我觉得不错。_____我一看价钱，_____是打六折，_____还得好几百块。_____我又去了几家商店，东西都很贵，_____，我什么都没买，就回家了。

1 結果	5 可是	9 昨天
2 我	6 所以	10 在那裡
3 雖然	7 後來	
4 可是	8 今天早上	

_____我在網上看見學校附近的購物中心有很多商店在打折。_____起床後我就開車去那個購物中心。_____，很多商店真的都打折，我很高興。_____想買一套運動服，_____走進了一家賣運動服的商店。進去一看，什麼都打六折，我覺得不錯。_____我一看價錢，_____是打六折，_____還得好幾百塊。_____我又去了幾家商店，東西都很貴。_____，我什麼都沒買，就回家了。

1 Q: Are you a history major?

_____

A: My major is not history but economics.

_____

2 Q: Are you a computer science Ph.D.?

_____

A: I'm not a computer science Ph.D. but a chemistry Ph.D.

_____

3 Q: Mom, are you against my marrying Little Wang?

_____

A: I'm not against it, but think it's too early for you to get married now. You'd better graduate from college before getting married.

_____

_____

4 Person A: I haven't seen your boyfriend Little Lin for a while. Did you fight?

_____

Person B: We didn't fight. He went to Mexico for study abroad and won't be back until next winter.

_____

Person A: So does that mean you broke up?

_____

Person B: We didn't break up. We chat online every single day.

_____

5   **Person A:**   Little Zhang, where did you say you'll have to take your son on Friday evening?

Person B: I'll have to take him to learn to swim. On Saturday I'll have to take him to a skating lesson.

Person A: I hope you get a day's rest on Sunday.

Person B: No, on Sunday I'll have to take my son to a piano lesson.

Person A: Your son is still just a kid. Won't he complain?

Person B: No, he loves learning these things. One moment he's learning this, and the other moment he's learning that. When we see how happy he is learning, we are happy, too.

6   **Person A:**   Little Gao, your older brother and sister-in-law are both teachers. Their opinions wouldn't differ in terms of education, right?

Person B: Although they are both teachers, their opinions often do differ when it comes to their child's education. My sister-in-law thinks that a child should play, but my brother wants their child to take this lesson or take that lesson.

Person A: Whose opinion do you agree with?

_____

Person B: I think both their views make sense. I think that when children play, they also learn. Is children's play learning? It depends on what you think learning is: you can learn many things from life, and of course you can also acquire a lot of knowledge from books and at school. I think my sister-in-law would definitely agree, because she is a teacher herself. But their child is only eight. He ought to play more.

_____

_____

_____

_____

_____

Person A: Then you agree with your sister-in-law!

_____

G Translate these passages into Chinese. **PRESENTATIONAL**

1 Many Chinese parents want their sons and daughters to become distinguished and successful like dragons and phoenixes. They hope that their children will be good students when they are young and will have successful careers later, so they put a lot of pressure on their children. However, Bai Xiaolin's (白小林) parents only hope that he will have a happy life. I don't think this is because they feel that Bai Xiaolin is incapable of being a good student or that he is incapable of having a great career in the future. On the contrary, it's because they feel that the most important thing in life is to be happy.

_____

_____

_____

_____

_____

2   The Chinese used to think that men must have their own career and women must be beautiful. Li Zhe's sister-in-law considers this kind of thinking very outdated. Nowadays, there are many women with master's and doctoral degrees who design and manage websites or are college professors. And why is it that men don't need to be good-looking? Li Zhe's older brother said it would be best for everyone to be as intelligent and good-looking as Li Zhe's sister-in-law.

_____

_____

_____

_____

_____

_____

3   Do you want your sons and daughters to become distinguished and successful like dragons and phoenixes? Do you want your children to have great careers? If you do, call us immediately! Our tutors can teach your children English, computer science, chemistry, piano, Chinese . . . Do not wait a moment longer. Hurry!

_____

_____

_____

_____

_____

_____

H   Design an after school or weekend program in Chinese that will, on the one hand, satisfy parents' desire to help their children live up to their full potential, and on the other hand, be enjoyable for the children. PRESENTATIONAL

I   Prepare a sales pitch to promote the program that you designed in (H). Make sure to entice both parents and their children by offering a variety of classes, reasonable fees, and flexible hours, and show that you can guarantee good results while letting children have fun at the same time. PRESENTATIONAL

J Write a story in Chinese based on the four images below. Make sure that your story has a beginning, middle, and end, and that the transition from one picture to the next is smooth and logical. PRESENTATIONAL

_____

_____

_____

_____

_____

中国地理

中國地理

Geography of China

✓ Check off the following language functions as you learn how to:

[ ] Compare basic geographic aspects of China and your own country

[ ] Describe features of a tourist sight that would attract or deter you

[ ] Name cities located in China's north, southeast, and south

[ ] Plan a trip to China, keeping in mind geography, climate, time, and budget

As you progress through the lesson, note other language functions you would like to learn.

_____

_____

_____

Audio

A Listen to the Textbook audio, then circle the most appropriate choice. INTERPRETIVE

1 Why do Zhang Tianming and Lisha study a map of China?

   a because they want to study abroad in China

   b because they plan to travel in China

   c because they have a geography test

2 Which Chinese city does Zhang Tianming suggest that they visit first?

   a Nanjing

   b Kunming

   c Beijing

3 According to Zhang Tianming, why is it not a good idea to visit Harbin?

   a It is too far away.

   b It is too cold.

   c He has been there before.

4 In which direction do most of the rivers in China flow?

   a southward

   b westward

   c eastward

5 What similarities do they see between China and the United States?

   a size and topography

   b population and topography

   c size and population

6 What are the reasons they finally decide to go to Yunnan?

   a its accessibility, pleasant weather, and ethnic diversity

   b its pleasant weather, attractive scenery, and ethnic diversity

   c its attractive scenery, accessibility, and ethnic diversity

B Listen to the Workbook Dialogue audio, then mark these statements true or false. INTERPRETIVE

1 _____ The speakers are planning a trip to Yunnan.

2 _____ According to the man, the weather in northern Yunnan is balmy all year round.

3 _____ The natural conditions in Yunnan are diverse.

4 _____ This conversation most likely takes place in October.

5 _____ According to the man, there are only two seasons in southern Yunnan.

6 _____ The man learned about Yunnan's climate in his geography class.

C   Listen to the Workbook Narrative 1 audio, then mark these statements true or false. **INTERPRETIVE**

1 ____   The speaker is a tour guide addressing tourists.

2 ____   They are going to visit a famous tourist sight.

3 ____   They will likely go to a Sichuanese or Hunanese restaurant for lunch.

D   Listen to the Workbook Narrative 2 audio, then mark these statements true or false. **INTERPRETIVE**

1 ____   The speaker is quite familiar with the person she is speaking to.

2 ____   According to the speaker, Harbin is hot in summer and cold in winter.

3 ____   The speaker encourages the other person to visit Harbin in winter to see the ice lanterns.

E   Listen to the Workbook Narrative 3 audio, then circle the most appropriate choice. **INTERPRETIVE**

1   Where did the speaker last talk to Teacher Wang?

     a   in Shanghai

     b   in New York

     c   in a western U.S. state

2   Which of the following is an accurate description of Teacher Wang?

     a   He doesn't know the U.S. well and has not traveled with the speaker.

     b   He knows the U.S. well but has not traveled with the speaker.

     c   He knows the U.S. well and has traveled with the speaker.

3   What is the speaker's impression of the western U.S.?

     a   The scenery is beautiful, but the tourist sights are crowded.

     b   The tourist sights are not very crowded, but the scenery is not very beautiful.

     c   The scenery is beautiful and the tourist sights are not very crowded.

4   Which of the cities is most likely to be on the speaker's itinerary next time he visits the U.S.?

     a   Washington, D.C.

     b   Los Angeles

     c   Chicago

F ____   Listen to the Workbook Listening Rejoinder audio. After hearing the first speaker, select the best response from the four choices given by the second speaker. Indicate the letter of your choice. **INTERPRETIVE**

A Compare the pronunciations of the underlined characters in the two words or phrases given. Provide their initials in *pinyin*.

<u>自</u>然 _____   四<u>季</u>如春 _____

B Compare the tones of the underlined characters in the two words or phrases given. Indicate the tones with 1 (first tone), 2 (second tone), 3 (third tone), 4 (fourth tone), or 0 (neutral tone).

到<u>处</u>/到<u>處</u> _____   相<u>处</u>/相<u>處</u> _____

III. Speaking

A Practice asking and answering these questions. Note: 国家/國家 means "country." **INTERPERSONAL**

1 你的家乡在你们国家的东部、西部、南部，还是北部？

   你的家鄉在你們國家的東部、西部、南部，還是北部？

2 北京是中国的首都和文化中心，上海是中国的经济中心。你们国家的首都是哪一个城市？你们国家的文化中心是哪一个城市？你们国家的经济中心是哪一个城市？

   北京是中國的首都和文化中心，上海是中國的經濟中心。你們國家的首都是哪一個城市？你們國家的文化中心是哪一個城市？你們國家的經濟中心是哪一個城市？

3 你们国家有高山吗？如果有，在哪里？

   你們國家有高山嗎？如果有，在哪裡？

4 你们国家最长的河流是哪条河？它是从哪边往哪边流？

   你們國家最長的河流是哪條河？它是從哪邊往哪邊流？

5 你们国家有沙漠吗？如果有，在哪里？

   你們國家有沙漠嗎？如果有，在哪裡？

Practice speaking with these prompts. PRESENTATIONAL

1 请简单介绍一下中国地理。

   請簡單介紹一下中國地理。

2 请比较一下你们国家和中国的地形、面积、人口。

   請比較一下你們國家和中國的地形、面積、人口。

3 If you have been to China, describe the city/province/region that impressed you the most, including its topography, climate, natural scenery, people, and food. If you have never been to China, name the city/province/region that you would most like to visit, and explain why you have chosen that place.

IV. Reading Comprehension

A Complete this section by writing the characters, *pinyin*, and English equivalent of each new word formed. Guess the meaning, then use a dictionary to confirm.

1 "冰灯"的"冰"+"人山人海"的"山"

   "冰燈"的"冰"+"人山人海"的"山"

   → 冰+山 → _____ _____ _____

2 "风景"的"景"+"颜色"的"色"

   "風景"的"景"+"顏色"的"色"

   → 景+色 → _____ _____ _____

3 "沙漠"的"沙"+"眼睛"的"眼"

   "沙漠"的"沙"+"眼睛"的"眼"

   → 沙+眼 → _____ _____ _____

4 "身体"的"体"+"面积"的"积"

   "身體"的"體"+"面積"的"積"

   → 体/體+积/積 → _____ _____ _____

5 “四倍多”的“倍”+“数字”的“数”

　　“四倍多”的“倍”+“數字”的“數”

　　→ 倍+数/數 → _____ _____ _____

6 “四季”的“季”+“过节”的“节”

　　“四季”的“季”+“過節”的“節”

　　→ 季+节/節 → _____ _____ _____

B Read this passage, then mark the statements true or false. INTERPRETIVE

　　中国人口多，喜欢旅游的人也越来越多。过节或者放假的时候，有名的旅游景点都是人山人海，挤得很。但是去中国旅游，不一定非去那几个最有名的地方不可。中国那么大，漂亮的地方和有意思的地方多极了。云南的西南部就有一个很特别的地方，那儿有很多少数民族，我们上次去那儿，他们都非常客气。那儿的自然风景特别美，天气也好，知道的人不多，所以一点儿也不挤。下次你去云南，一定要去那儿看看。那儿虽然离飞机场非常远，可是坐火车和汽车很方便。

　　中國人口多，喜歡旅遊的人也越來越多。過節或者放假的時候，有名的旅遊景點都是人山人海，擠得很。但是去中國旅遊，不一定非去那幾個最有名的地方不可。中國那麼大，漂亮的地方和有意思的地方多極了。雲南的西南部就有一個很特別的地方，那兒有很多少數民族，我們上次去那兒，他們都非常客氣。那兒的自然風景特別美，天氣也好，知道的人不多，所以一點兒也不擠。下次你去雲南，一定要去那兒看看。那兒雖然離飛機場非常遠，可是坐火車和汽車很方便。

1 ____ The author wants to visit Yunnan because he/she has never been there.

2 ____ The author suggests that the more frequently visited tourist attractions are more beautiful.

3 _____ The passage mentions a place that is becoming a major tourist attraction.

4 _____ That place in Yunnan has beautiful scenery and nice weather.

5 _____ That place is easily accessible by train, but not by plane.

C Read this passage, then mark the statements true or false. INTERPRETIVE

　　蓝天旅游公司欢迎您参加我们的旅游计划。很多人都觉得过中国新年应该回家，待在家里。但是，新年我们有一个多星期的假，是最好的旅游时间，为什么非在家里过年不可呢？我们这里冬天自然条件不太好，非常冷，为什么不去南边走走？为什么不去看看广州和深圳，去看看大海，或者去看看四季如春的云南？大家不用担心飞机票太贵，因为航空公司会给我们打七折。如果您对去中国南部旅游有兴趣，请赶快给我们打电话。我们一定会给您和您的家人安排一个非常特别的新年假期。

　　藍天旅遊公司歡迎您參加我們的旅遊計劃。很多人都覺得過中國新年應該回家，待在家裡。但是，新年我們有一個多星期的假，是最好的旅遊時間，為什麼非在家裡過年不可呢？我們這裡冬天自然條件不太好，非常冷，為什麼不去南邊走走？為什麼不去看看廣州和深圳，去看看大海，或者去看看四季如春的雲南？大家不用擔心飛機票太貴，因為航空公司會給我們打七折。如果您對去中國南部旅遊有興趣，請趕快給我們打電話。我們一定會給您和您的家人安排一個非常特別的新年假期。

1 _____ This message is from a tourist agency.

2 _____ Residents of Guangzhou and Shenzhen are the intended audience of this message.

3 _____ According to the message, those who sign up will get airplane tickets at favorable prices.

4 _____ Weather conditions at the destinations mentioned are a major selling point of this message.

5 _____ Interested people should go online to sign up.

D Look at this weather forecast, then answer the question in English. INTERPRETIVE

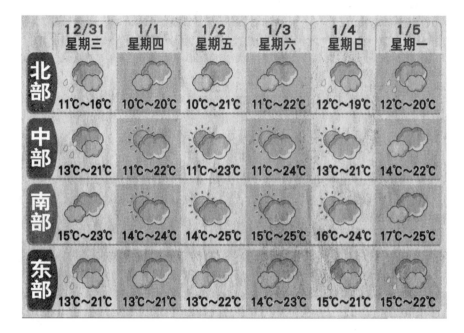

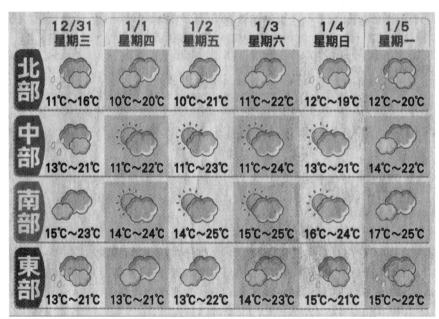

1 On average, which region has the coldest weather?

_____

E Look at this newspaper advertisement, then answer the questions in English. INTERPRETIVE

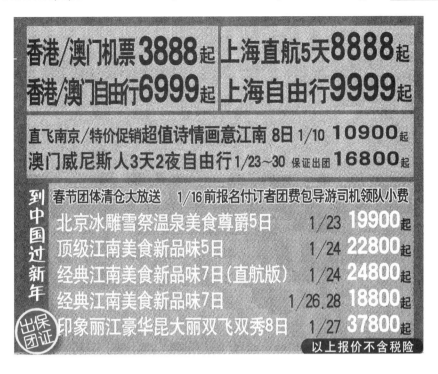

1 What destination cities are offered? List at least four.

_____

2 What time of year will these tours depart?

_____

3 What do 直航 and 自由行 mean?

_____

Look at this advertisement, then answer the questions in English. **INTERPRETIVE**

云南	四星纯玩-昆明.大理.丽江双飞双汽6日丽江含小索道	3060
	昆明.大理.丽江.泸沽湖/香格里拉　　　双飞双卧8日	2510起
	昆明.大理.丽江.版纳(野象谷)　三飞一卧7/四飞一卧8日	3230起
	昆明.大理.丽江.中甸豪华品质团　四星+五星　双飞双汽8日	3380
	昆明.大理.丽江.虎跳峡豪华纯玩团　四星+五星　三飞6日	4030
海南	四星纯玩（含蜈支洲或南山）　　　　双飞5日	2100起
	海洋任我游2日行程+2日自由　三亚往返　五星住宿　双飞5日	2350
	三亚4晚5天自由人（机票+自选3-5星酒店 单订特价机票）	2300起
新疆	乌鲁木齐.土鲁番.葡萄沟.天山天池.敦煌.月牙泉.嘉峪关.兰州　双飞6日	3500
	乌鲁木齐.土鲁番.葡萄沟.天山天池.魔鬼城.布尔津.喀纳斯　双飞7日	3750

雲南	四星純玩-昆明.大理.麗江雙飛雙汽6日麗江含小索道	3060
	昆明.大理.麗江.瀘沽湖/香格里拉　　雙飛雙臥8日	2510起
	昆明.大理.麗江.版納(野象谷)三飛一臥7／四飛一臥8日	3230起
	昆明.大理.麗江.中甸豪華品質團　四星+五星　雙飛雙汽8日	3380
	昆明.大理.麗江.虎跳峽豪華純玩團　四星+五星　三飛6日	4030
海南	四星純玩(含蜈支洲或南山)　　　　雙飛5日	2100起
	海洋任我游2日行程+2日自由　三亞往返　五星住宿　雙飛5日	2350
	三亞4晚5天自由人(機票+自選3-5星酒店　單訂特價機票)	2300起
新疆	烏魯木齊.土魯番.葡萄溝.天山天池.敦煌.月牙泉.嘉峪關.蘭州　雙飛6日	3500
	烏魯木齊.土魯番.葡萄溝.天山天池.魔鬼城.布爾津.喀納斯　雙飛7日	3750

1 How many tours are heading to Yunnan?

_____

2 Among the Yunnan tours, which one would you prefer? Why?

_____

3 What do 飞/飛, 汽, and 五星 mean in English?

_____

A Form a character by combining the given components as indicated. Then use that character in a word, phrase, or short sentence.

1 左边一个三点水，右边一个"可以"的"可"，

左邊一個三點水，右邊一個"可以"的"可"，

是 ＿＿＿＿＿＿ 的 ＿＿＿ 。

2 上边一个"少"，下边一个"目"，

上邊一個"少"，下邊一個"目"，

是 ＿＿＿＿＿＿ 的 ＿＿＿ 。

3 左边一个三点水，右边一个"打工"的"工"，

左邊一個三點水，右邊一個"打工"的"工"，

是 ＿＿＿＿＿＿ 的 ＿＿＿ 。

4 左边一个"土"，右边一个"四川"的"川"，

左邊一個"土"，右邊一個"四川"的"川"，

是 ＿＿＿＿＿＿ 的 ＿＿＿ 。

B Locate the following cities on the map by placing the corresponding numbers next to their locations. INTERPRETIVE

1 广州/廣州   4 北京   7 深圳

2 哈尔滨/哈爾濱   5 天津

3 南京   6 上海

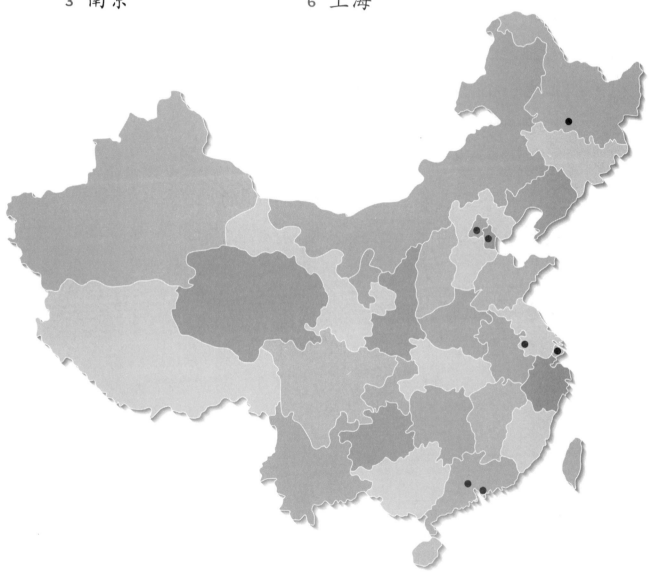

c   Fill in the blanks with either 因为/因為 or 为了/為了. <u>INTERPRETIVE</u>

1   _____研究中国的少数民族，王教授在云南待了一年半。

    _____研究中國的少數民族，王教授在雲南待了一年半。

2   _____新年假期旅游景点人太多，小李决定不出门，在家休息。

    _____新年假期旅遊景點人太多，小李決定不出門，在家休息。

3   _____了解美国地理，张先生买了一张新地图。

    _____了解美國地理，張先生買了一張新地圖。

4   _____让女儿将来能做出一番大事业，李太太从小就让女儿学这学那。

    _____讓女兒將來能做出一番大事業，李太太從小就讓女兒學這學那。

5   _____减轻父母的经济负担，张天明想打工挣钱。

    _____減輕父母的經濟負擔，張天明想打工掙錢。

6   _____张天明整天离不开电脑，大家觉得他玩儿电脑玩儿上瘾了。

    _____張天明整天離不開電腦，大家覺得他玩兒電腦玩兒上瘾了。

D Give an account of what the IC characters like to do based on the visual clues. Use 而 in your answers, following the example below. PRESENTATIONAL

柯林喜欢上网聊天儿，而林雪梅喜欢打电话聊天儿。
柯林喜歡上網聊天兒，而林雪梅喜歡打電話聊天兒。

1

_____

2

_____

3

_____

4

_____

Answer the questions based on the clues provided, following the example below.

Q: 什么时候去北京好？ (autumn)
　　什麼時候去北京好？

A: 秋天去北京最好不过了。
　　秋天去北京最好不過了。

1 Q: 张天明的母亲觉得他念什么合适？ (finance)
　　　張天明的母親覺得他念什麼合適？

A: _____ 。

2 Q: 母亲节快到了，送什么礼物给妈妈好？ (flowers)
　　　母親節快到了，送什麼禮物給媽媽好？

A: _____ 。

3 Q: 下学期选什么课轻松？ (drawing)
　　　下學期選什麼課輕鬆？

A: _____ 。

F Connect the following individual sentences into a coherent narrative by adding connecting devices, deleting unnecessary pronouns and other repetitive elements, and changing the punctuation marks as appropriate. INTERPRETIVE & PRESENTATIONAL

1 去年寒假我跟女朋友去中国旅行。
　　去年寒假我跟女朋友去中國旅行。

2 我们12月15号坐飞机去北京。
　　我們12月15號坐飛機去北京。

3 我们18号坐火车去哈尔滨。
　　我們18號坐火車去哈爾濱。

4 我们在哈尔滨看了冰灯，冰灯漂亮极了。
　　我們在哈爾濱看了冰燈，冰燈漂亮極了。

5 我们22号从哈尔滨一下子到了南方的广州。
　　我們22號從哈爾濱一下子到了南方的廣州。

6 广州比哈尔滨暖和多了。
　　廣州比哈爾濱暖和多了。

7 广州有很多花，很漂亮。
　　廣州有很多花，很漂亮。

8 我和女朋友24号回她南京老家。
　　我和女朋友24號回她南京老家。

9 女朋友的父母看见我好像很高兴。
　　女朋友的父母看見我好像很高興。

10 我们在女朋友家过了新年。
　　我們在女朋友家過了新年。

11 1月3号我们回到美国。
　　1月3號我們回到美國。

G Translate these sentences into Chinese. PRESENTATIONAL

1 Chinese New Year is coming. There are beginning to be more and more people in shopping centers and restaurants.

_____

_____

2 Professor Wang was very interested in this issue. As soon as he got home, he started to read up on the issue.

_____

_____

3 Little Lin plans to go to graduate school after graduation, and doesn't plan to work.

_____

_____

4 My father likes to eat spicy (things), and my mother likes to eat sweet (things).

_____

_____

H Translate these sentences into Chinese. PRESENTATIONAL

1 Person A: Are you busy next week?

_____

Person B: Monday, I have a piano lesson; Tuesday, I have a swimming lesson; Wednesday . . .

_____

Person A: OK, OK. You sound busy. Never mind, I'll ask someone else to dinner.

_____

2 Person A: Where would you like to travel this winter? Let's go to Harbin, OK?

_____

Person B: Harbin's ice lanterns are very famous, but it's too cold.

_____

Person A: Then let's go to the south, to Hainan (海南).

_____

Person B: Hainan is fun, but too many people go sightseeing there.

_____

Person A: How do you feel about going to Yunnan? It's neither too cold nor too hot, and there are not too many tourists.

_____

_____

Person B: Many places in Yunnan are spring-like throughout the year. It's a great place to visit.

_____

3 Person A: So that means you agree to go to Yunnan?

_____

Person B: The only thing is it's too far away.

_____

Person A: Now I know: you are a traveler who likes to sit at home.

_____

4 **Person A:** Have you been to Nanjing? Is Nanjing a fun place?

_____

Person B: Yes, I have. Nanjing is a really fun place with a very long history. It's by the Yangtze River and has great natural conditions.

_____

_____

Person A: What about the landscape?

_____

Person B: The landscape is very beautiful, too.

_____

Person A: Do you want to go to Nanjing again?

_____

Person B: Yes. My parents were born and grew up in Nanjing.

_____

Person A: Then let's go this summer.

_____

Person B: Nanjing is too hot in the summer. We'd better go in the spring or in the fall.

_____

Translate these passages into Chinese. PRESENTATIONAL

1 There are tall mountains as well as plateaus in Yunnan. Therefore, geographical conditions differ greatly. Everywhere, the landscape is very beautiful. In many places, no matter when you go it's neither too cold nor too hot. It is very suitable for tourism.

_____

_____

_____

_____

_____

2 America's topography is very similar to China's, Its land area is about the same as well. However, the population is only a quarter (四分之一) of China's [population]. In America's southwest there are also tall mountains, plateaus, and deserts, and the landscape is beautiful. I hear that during holidays, tourist sights are also crowded with people.

_____

_____

_____

_____

_____

3 The population of China's northeast is smaller than that of the southeast. There is a big plain, and winter there is very cold. Harbin's ice lanterns are often mentioned on TV. That is why many people in China know about them.

_____

_____

_____

_____

J Do some research and complete the sentences. Proper nouns can be written in English. If you like a challenge and don't mind a bit more work, then you can fill in the names in Chinese. **INTERPRETIVE**

1 世界上最大的沙漠是 _____ 。

世界上最大的沙漠是 _____ 。

2 世界上最高的山是 _____ 。

世界上最高的山是 _____ 。

3 世界上最高的高原是 _____ 。

世界上最高的高原是 _____ 。

4 世界上最长的河流是 _____ 。

世界上最長的河流是 _____ 。

5 世界上人口最多的国家是 _____ 。

世界上人口最多的國家是 _____ 。

K Write an introduction to your hometown or the place where you currently live. Include information such as where it is located within the state or the country, whether there are mountains, rivers, plateaus, deserts, or plains nearby, and the size of its population. **PRESENTATIONAL**

L Choose 四川, 新疆, 云南/雲南, or 广东/廣東 and write an introduction to it. Find out where it is located within China, what topographical features it has, what the climate is like, what kind of cuisine it is famous for, etc. **PRESENTATIONAL**

M Write a story based on the four images below. Make sure your story has a beginning, middle, and end, and that the transition from one picture to the next is smooth and logical. PRESENTATIONAL

1)

2)

3)

4)

Bringing It Together (Lessons 6–10)

I. Checking Your Pronunciation

A Write down the correct pronunciation, including tones, of the following short sentences in *pinyin*. Use a computer or smartphone to record yourself speaking. If you've been asked to do so, send the recording to your teacher. Then translate each sentence into English.

1 吵架解决不了问题。

　吵架解決不了問題。

_____

_____

2 说不定他们真的分手了。

　說不定他們真的分手了。

_____

_____

3 母亲根本不看网络新闻。

　母親根本不看網絡新聞。

_____

_____

4 这个软件已经落伍了。

　這個軟件已經落伍了。

_____

_____

5 他老是玩电脑，结果玩上瘾了。
   他老是玩電腦，結果玩上癮了。

   _____

   _____

6 她收入少，经济负担重。
   她收入少，經濟負擔重。

   _____

   _____

7 花钱容易挣钱难。
   花錢容易掙錢難。

   _____

   _____

8 农村孩子可以受到良好的教育。
   農村孩子可以受到良好的教育。

   _____

   _____

9 很多人认为打工影响学习。
   很多人認為打工影響學習。

   _____

   _____

10 她希望取得硕士和博士学位。

她希望取得碩士和博士學位。

_____

_____

11 家长应该尊重孩子的选择。

家長應該尊重孩子的選擇。

_____

_____

12 旅行的路线已经决定了。

旅行的路線已經決定了。

_____

_____

13 沙漠中看不到河流。

沙漠中看不到河流。

_____

_____

14 云南有些地方四季如春。

雲南有些地方四季如春。

_____

_____

A While studying abroad in China, you run into the following scenarios. PRESENTATIONAL

1 You're setting up a blind date for a Chinese friend. Who among your acquaintances would make a good match? Make a compatibility list.

_____

_____

_____

2 As a WeChat convert, you want to convince your friends how useful and helpful WeChat and other Chinese apps can be for daily life. What reasons might be on your list?

_____

_____

_____

3 Your Chinese friends have asked you to explain how American students finance their education. Write down three points you would make.

_____

_____

_____

4 You need to recruit some Chinese tutors for an American school. Prepare a flyer explaining the qualifications you are looking for.

_____

_____

_____

5 You are asked to promote tourism for your hometown. Prepare a simple brochure describing the landscape and climate of your hometown.

_____

_____

_____

Engage in some personal brainstorming and fill out the provided lists in Chinese. After you've finished, compare notes with one of your classmates. **PRESENTATIONAL & INTERPERSONAL**

1 How would you describe your personality traits? What do you like about yourself? What would you like to change about yourself?

Likes: _____

_____

Changes: _____

_____

2 Explain what you like and don't like about the Internet.

Likes: _____

_____

Dislikes: _____

_____

3 List some personal choices that you think could save money and some others that could waste money.

Save money: _____

_____

Waste money: _____

_____

4 List things that you think a parent should and should not do to give a child a balanced childhood.

Should do: _____

_____

Should not do: _____

_____

5   List features that would attract you to or deter you from visiting a tourist destination.

Attractive features: _____

_____

Deterrent features: _____

_____

After you have finished filling out your lists, interview a classmate about his/her opinions on these topics.

C Based on, but not limited to, the information you provided in (A) and (B) of this section, present an oral report or write a paragraph in Chinese in response to each of the following questions.
PRESENTATIONAL

1   Your friends are trying to find you a boyfriend or girlfriend. What would you tell them to ensure they find a good match for you?

2   You are asked to comment on the impact the Internet has had on people's daily lives. What would you say?

3   You are asked to talk to high school and college students on how they can live within their means and be financially responsible. What would you say?

4   You are an educator. What would be your advice to parents on how to give their children a happy childhood while preparing them for their future careers?

5   You are a tour guide planning to lead a one-month trip to China in the winter. What route would you choose, what places would you visit, and what do you need to know about those places?